One Hundred and One Devotions
for Homeschool Moms

To My Sweet Sister Shannon,
My inspiration for
homeschooling.

Love,
Sandy

CROSSWAY BOOKS BY JACKIE WELLWOOD

The Busy Mom's Guide to Simple Living

One Hundred and One Devotions for Homeschool Moms

ONE HUNDRED AND ONE

Devotions for Homeschool Moms

Jackie Wellwood

CROSSWAY BOOKS • WHEATON, ILLINOIS

A DIVISION OF GOOD NEWS PUBLISHERS

Cover design: Cindy Kiple

Cover illustration: Pierre Auguste Renoir/Super Stock

Second printing, 2000

Printed in the United States of America

The Scripture passages are taken from the King James Version.

Library of Congress Cataloging-in-Publication Data
Wellwood, Jackie, 1959–
    One Hundred and One devotions for homeschool moms / Jackie Wellwood.
        p.   cm.
    ISBN 1-58134-139-3 (trade pbk. : alk. paper)
    1. Mothers Prayer-books and devotions—English. 2. Home schooling Prayer-books and devotions—English. I. Title. II. Title: One hundred and one devotions for homeschool moms. III. Title: One hundred and one devotions for homeschool moms.
    BV4847.W45 2000
    242'.6431—dc21   99-42493
                                                CIP

15	14	13	12	11	10	09	08	07	06	05	04	03	02	01	00
15	14	13	12	11	10	9	8	7	6	5	4	3	2		

TABLE OF CONTENTS

ACKNOWLEDGMENTS

*J*ust saying thank you hardly seems enough for my loving family who made it possible for me to write this book. We would not have eaten had it not been for the diligent efforts that Jamie made in the kitchen. The rest of the children—Jenny, Jimmy, Jonathan, Joanna, Josiah, and Julianne—all played their roles to keep things running. My husband, Jim, made the biggest sacrifice as he lost his wife for a while. It's okay; I'm back.

Thank you also to my friend Karen for her input and encouragement as I learned that I was moving from the neighborhood right in the middle of my writing.

Thank you to my pastor and his wife, Dr. and Mrs. S. M. Davis, who proofread the manuscript.

Thank you to Mrs. "B" who gave me much-needed wisdom and insight as I finished writing this book.

Thank you to my editor, Lila Bishop, for improving the manuscript with her helpful changes.

Thank you most of all to my heavenly Father who allowed challenging circumstances to heighten my depth of understanding as I was writing. In the midst of full days where I could hardly think, the words were there. Only God could have blessed me so richly.

PREFACE

*I*t is not easy for a mother to find time to write a book. Nursing a baby, training a two-year-old, and suddenly moving to a farm all made writing nearly impossible at times. So it was during the writing of this devotional. I was in the process of recovering from my most difficult pregnancy and delivery. I wrote this book during the most stressful time I have ever experienced in my life.

God was good. He showed me my weak areas. I saw problems in my life I had not noticed before. I was saddened at the realization that I sin with my tongue often. I know what I should do, but I am not successfully doing it. If it is true that the way you behave under pressure is the way you really are, then I have so much more to learn about life. I have much to learn about people—especially those in my immediate family. I need to grow spiritually if I am to be the woman that God wants me to be.

Spiritual growth is the purpose of this devotional. I wrote it for me even though I believe it will help you, too. I wanted a book for my bedside table that would minister to the unique circumstances that I face as a homeschool mom. My problems are not unusual. The anecdotes may not be what you have experienced, but surely you can relate to the topics. The Lord has a plan for each of us. It is my desire that your walk with Jesus be strengthened through spending time at His feet so you can better understand His plan for you. These devotions are only a catalyst to draw you closer to the Master.

Allow yourself to become close—very close to Jesus. He will show you what you need to refine, just as He did for me. It is painful, but it is the only way to be the very best homeschool mom that you can be.

1

A MEEK AND QUIET SPIRIT

But let it be the hidden man of the heart, in that which is not corruptible, even the ornament of a meek and quiet spirit, which is in the sight of God of great price.

1 PETER 3:4

I have been looking for a meek and quiet spirit ever since I found out about it. This spirit seems to be hard to find, and I'm not sure that I have seen it much. I want one very badly. I am not by nature a meek person. If quiet is the opposite of loud, then I don't think I am quiet by nature either. Since I can't find a meek and quiet spirit, it looks like I will have to develop one. This could take some work.

My understanding of the word *meek* is that it is mild, not prone to being provoked, not easily irritated, and forbearing when mistreated. *Quiet* means still, peaceful, calm, and not troubled. I know I have evidenced these character qualities quite frequently—in my sleep. When I am awake, I don't know where they go. But I do know *why* they go.

I respond to my circumstances. Most of us do. For a long time I thought that if I remained calm and kept my mouth shut when someone was aggravating me, I would have a meek and quiet spirit. I managed to do this a couple of times, but I felt unsettled because I was still rather charged up on the inside. Even though I did not say what I was thinking, my thoughts were still wrong. I did not feel peaceful because my insides were in turmoil. I still allowed myself to be provoked, even though nobody knew it. This isn't true meekness; it's just faking it.

A meek and quiet spirit stays calm and peaceful on the *inside* as well as on the *outside* during a time of disturbance. Are we calm and even while injustices fly in our face, or are we just about to boil over? A meek and quiet spirit won't respond to the situation immediately. After the passion and fury of the moment subside, then a calm and collected response can be given. Our souls can remain quiet during times of provocation. Our mouths must remain still and our thoughts kept to ourselves. I told you this would take some work.

Do you desire a meek and quiet spirit? It is God's best for us.

PRAYER

Father, You know I am a complete failure in this area. I need to be completely overhauled in this department. I understand how to stay calm on the outside even though I don't always do it. I do not understand how to stay unruffled on the inside. Only You can take me to this new height. I know this transformation will be life-changing. PLEASE help me to take these character qualities of Yours into my own character. I need them badly.

FOOD FOR THOUGHT

1. What circumstances provoke you to speak inappropriately to another person? How can you eliminate or reduce the frequency of these circumstances?

2. Practice remaining calm when someone is agitating you. Have a close friend say words to you that incite you to anger. Remain calm and even during this drill.

3. Train your children in meekness. Role-play situations that could make them angry. Teach them to respond in a godly fashion.

2

HOUSE BEAUTIFUL?

Set your affection on things above, not on things on the earth.

COLOSSIANS 3:2

◈

I finally figured out why my house looks "lived in." It is very simple. We live in it. All nine of us—most of the time. My husband's work schedule allows him to be home more than he is away at work. This means that we must keep track of two adults and seven children from morning until night in our home.

Although we have a place for almost everything, we are still in the process of training our children to put everything in its place. While we try to minimize our clutter, it creeps in daily. Although we have regular tasks that we all perform to keep our home clean, some of us are still learning how to do our tasks.

I could get discouraged by the "lived-in" look in our home. I could work harder to prevent that look. But why? The only way our house stays tidy is if we clean up and then leave for the day. How could we *home*school if we are never home?

I confess that I gave up on my old standard of a "clean" house long ago. I don't want my children to be restricted from living in their own home during the early years when they are learning to pick up after themselves. How else would they learn to clean up if there never was any mess? I make messes myself. They happen when I am being productive. The best solution I have is just to clean up when I am done. If multiple children are being productive in your home, then you might as well expect some pretty big messes.

The word *affection* in Colossians 3:2 is the key to understanding how to handle these messes. Your affection is what is important to you. I would rather that my children learn to serve by cleaning up after themselves than have a clean house because they aren't allowed to mess it up. I would rather spend my time teaching them biblical truths than taking the time myself to clean everything up that they miss each time.

Have you considered where you put your affection? Is it on that which lasts for eternity, or is it on temporal matters on this earth?

PRAYER

Lord, keep me ever mindful that the attention and work I put into training my children is of lasting value. The house gets dirty again. The clutter and disorganization return. Help me to keep these responsibilities secondary to the training of my children. May I remember to teach them how to clean up after themselves as preparation for the rest of their lives. ✒

FOOD FOR THOUGHT

1. What aspect of your home is the most difficult to keep clean and orderly?
2. Will this problem correct itself when your children are a little older? If not, do you need to change your attitude toward this problem?
3. Make a list of what you consider to have eternal value. Make another list of what you consider to be important only here on earth. What does this tell you about setting your priorities regarding the condition of your home?

AUTHOR'S NOTE: I am in no way endorsing a messy house. Order is important but must be balanced with other considerations, particularly if your children are in your home with you throughout the day.

3

TOO MANY HATS

And Jesus answered and said unto her, Martha, Martha,
thou art careful and troubled about many things: But one thing
is needful; and Mary hath chosen that good part,
which shall not be taken away from her.

LUKE 10:41-42

I can't remember when it all got so complicated. It started out pretty manageable. I began learning how to be a good wife. Then I started to pursue the joys of mothering. Feeling somewhat competent in these areas (most of the time anyway), I then plunged wholeheartedly into training to be a teacher of my children in my home. Mostly I read everything I could find on the subject. I talked to women who seemed to homeschool with ease.

Then, all of a sudden, my roles began to expand—exponentially. I had the distinct feeling that I was wearing too many hats. Worse yet, I had to fill some of these roles all at the same time. The baby needed to be nursed during a spelling test at the same moment the four-year-old needed assistance in the bathroom. At that time I was already half an hour behind on lunch preparations. My husband called to see how my day was going, and I didn't respond like a good wife. The phone rang, the dryer beeped, and I quit. No, not really. But don't you wonder sometimes what role you should fill first?

My experience in the business world taught me to prioritize and do the most important items on the list first. At times I don't even have a chance to make a list now. I don't see how I can focus on doing the most important thing first when I have to do many important things simultaneously. It frustrates me to leave some things undone, because it just doesn't seem to be the right thing to do. Or is it?

The story of Mary and Martha addresses this question. Luke 10:38-42 illustrates an important truth for us as we seek a sane solution to the demands of life. As Jesus visited the home of Mary and Martha, there were preparations to make. While Mary listened to Jesus, Martha was busy with the details. When Martha shows irritation at her sister for leaving all the work to her, Jesus responds, "Martha, Martha . . . thou art careful and troubled about many things: But one thing is needful; and Mary hath chosen that good part, which shall not be taken away from her" (Luke 10:41-42). Mary was sitting at Jesus' feet, listening. He tells Martha that this is the best thing to do.

Do I seek Jesus to direct me in the roles that I must fill at a given moment? Do I listen to God regarding what role He wants me to fill?

PRAYER

Lord, help me to hear Your wise direction for my day. Teach me to say yes to the best You have for me. Let me clearly understand Your plan for the division of my time and effort. ❧

FOOD FOR THOUGHT

1. Which of my roles is the most demanding?

2. Is there anything I can do to simplify this role and make the job easier each day? How?

3. What would help me the most to be faithful in daily Bible reading so that I am spending time at Jesus' feet?

4

FUZZY TIME

Create in me a clean heart, O God;
and renew a right spirit within me.

PSALM 51:10

*M*y little Julianne had many a fussy moment during her first six months
of life. I called them her "fuzzy times." She got "fuzzy" quite often for a time
and required some extra attention. I noticed that her mother also had "fuzzy
times." I could be described as crabby, irritated, annoyed, unsteady, and
other things that sound much worse. During a time of great pressure I asked
my husband to hold my hand when I started to get fuzzed up. He would
not let go until I stopped being "fuzzy." This helped a little but did not solve
the problem.

Have you ever tried to get yourself out of a bad mood? I have. It is difficult. When my spirit is not sweet, I have never been successful at realigning
myself. It is God who renews the right spirit in me. God creates the clean
heart, not me. Unless I take the initiative to seek God, it won't happen.

In the midst of a trying time, make time to spend alone with God. A daily
devotion may not be enough. Multiple quiet moments might be required during periods of stress. Seek the Lord first to renew a right spirit. All other efforts
will fall short if this critical first step is omitted.

Prayer has helped me the most during "fuzzy times." I must confess
sins that I have committed (usually with my mouth) and ask forgiveness
and cleansing. Seek the Holy Spirit for direction and insight into God's Word.
Pray for understanding of problems and their solutions using biblical princi-

ples. Confess your sins to those you have sinned against (husbands too!) and ask for their forgiveness. Do this as often as necessary on a "fuzzy" day. Humble yourself no matter what it takes.

Homeschooling is a demanding undertaking. If we are not careful to prepare spiritually for each day, we will experience much "fuzzy time." Find that quiet time with the Lord. You can't afford not to. Allow God's Word to fill you so that you are not provoked by the annoyances of the day. Let the Holy Spirit guide you through situations that you would respond to badly on your own. Take comfort in knowing that God can and will restore a right spirit within you. Seek only Him to do just that.

Are you "fuzzy" today? Get on your knees right now.

PRAYER

Dear Lord, I know what I need to do, but I don't do it. I don't faithfully spend quiet time with You daily. Little ones waking me at night make it hard to get up early. Late at night I can hardly hold my head up. My personal devotions are too sporadic. Therefore my "fuzzy times" seem worse than the baby's. Oh, what a state I am in! Prompt me before I get irritated to stop and take a quiet time. You are my all in all and will do as You promise. Forgive me for not giving You enough of my time. I am ashamed, but I receive Your forgiveness and Your grace this moment. ✎

FOOD FOR THOUGHT

1. When your spirit is not right, is it because you have not had a daily quiet time with the Lord?

2. Do you admit to any and all sins you commit during a "fuzzy time"? Humble yourself before your family and God.

3. Memorize Psalm 51:10.

5

I CAN DO IT MYSELF!

Not that we are sufficient of ourselves to think any thing as of ourselves; but our sufficiency is of God.

2 CORINTHIANS 3:5

❧

*M*y first thoughts as a new homeschooler were that if I could learn more about how to homeschool, then I would certainly be able to manage it. I tend to be the self-reliant type and didn't view homeschooling much differently than I did classes in college: Get the book, read the material, show my comprehension by getting a good grade on the test. I really believed that getting the right curriculum, organizing my school area efficiently, and setting up a workable schedule would be all that I would need to be successful.

Initially this did work quite well. But over time as more students were born into our school and the demands of homeschooling grew, the error in my thinking became obvious. The Bible is the foundational curriculum for us, and all other material is supplemental in the training of our children. How unfortunate that I as their teacher and mother had missed such an important truth found in their core curriculum.

I am in no way sufficient to homeschool my children by myself. There isn't enough preparation, books, time, or anything else that could change my insufficiency. No matter how prepared I am, I cannot do this myself! No matter how organized I am, I cannot do this myself! No matter how easily my children learn, I cannot do this myself!

Sometimes our days are smooth sailing, and I wonder what the big deal is anyway. Other days are very demanding, and I seem to just be getting through them. Either type of day requires our reliance on God, not on ourselves. Bad days especially demand the perspective and guidance only our loving Father can offer to us.

Have you been relying on yourself to keep your homeschool running smoothly? Are you comfortable doing it alone?

PRAYER

Heavenly Father, please forgive my self-reliance. I try to do so much on my own. I study methods and materials before I study Your Word. Forgive me for putting more faith in my ability to manage our homeschool than in Your ability and desire to equip me for the task. Keep me ever mindful that without You this task is impossible. ❧

FOOD FOR THOUGHT

1. Have you found yourself depending on your own efforts to make your homeschool the best it can be? If so, what problems have you encountered?

2. Are you uncomfortable letting go of some of the daily details and allowing God to give you what you need to be successful? This discomfort could be the starting place for a closer walk with the Lord if you yield this area of your school to Him.

3. Make a list of all of the areas in your life where you feel confident in your own ability (example: selecting next year's curriculum, making sure all of your children have adequate clothing, choosing a birthday present your husband will enjoy). Next to each item, write the words "God has enabled me to be successful in this area!" Spend some quiet time praising the Lord for all that He has enabled you to accomplish. Ask Him to continue to be by your side in all future endeavors.

6

JOYFUL MOTHER

*He maketh the barren woman to keep house, and to be
a joyful mother of children. Praise ye the Lord.*

PSALM 113:9

✑

*C*ultural norms don't necessarily make us feel that motherhood is a joy. Comments from strangers that I sure have my hands full don't usually spark joy in my heart. They are right—I do have my hands full. It isn't always easy, and most often it is a challenge. People frequently question our family size and wonder why I would *want* to have my children home with me all day. Inevitably August comes, and I begin to hear familiar comments from mothers about how happy they are that their children are going back to school. They certainly did not feel much joy in spending the summer with their children.

I suffer from the same malady—lack of joy. I get caught up in the nitty-gritty details of each day, and if I am not careful, I miss all of the joy that my children can bring me daily. Recently I have been making a point of stopping to observe my children. Josiah, the two-year-old, was playing in the living room with a little toy tractor. As he pushed the toy, he pushed out his bottom lip and made the cutest face. I was glad I had seen this and smiled, because a lot of his other antics have not made me smile.

Lack of joy is rooted in ingratitude for the circumstances we find ourselves in. Count it a blessing that your children are underfoot all day and you can see everything that happens as they grow. Be happy to know that when your teenager has a problem that needs to be talked about, you are nearby for such an important task. Realize the magnitude of the ministry that the Lord has given you in training your children at home. Enjoy these precious days that older women keep telling me are the best days of my life.

Our joy is in being there each day to train our children—not in achieving some high standard of performance each day. Joy comes when we allow ourselves to *be* a joyful mother of children instead of *doing* all the tasks we think we must do. True joy is accepting God's best for us.

Have you found joy in being with your children today? Have you praised God for the children He has entrusted to your care?

PRAYER

Dear Jesus, I am grateful to You for the precious children You have graciously given to me. Forgive me for my impatience with their childish behavior. Help me to see the beauty in their daily development. Show me where to look for joy in each day no matter what the circumstances. Thank You for my children. ❧

FOOD FOR THOUGHT

1. Have I accepted my role as a homeschool mom and embraced the calling as my ministry? Why or why not? Does this bring me joy?
2. What are the joy-stealers in my life?
3. Take a piece of paper and number it from 1 to 25. List ways your children bring you joy. Make another list of ten ways the children could bring you more joy if you relaxed a little and let yourself *be* a mother instead of *doing* so much (example: sit down and let a child tell you what he or she is thinking).

7

DISCOURAGED

Casting all your care upon him; for he careth for you.

1 PETER 5:7

⤐

We have placed an emphasis on character training since the beginning of our homeschooling ten years ago. Inappropriate attitudes and comments between the children are watched for and addressed as consistently as possible. We do not allow our children to treat each other in a rude manner. We, as husband and wife, try to be good role models for our children. Our shelves are lined with good character-building stories.

With all of this wonderful preparation, I daily struggle with relational problems between my children. My daughters are often in a competition with one another that leads to bickering. My darling sons play a game of who can aggravate the other one the most. My little ones act like babies (this is fine since they are babies, but screaming for a cookie still gets on my nerves).

After spending so much time training for godly character, I am disappointed that we have so many problems. This is discouraging to me because I feel that I must be doing something wrong. Maybe I wasn't consistent enough (this is a problem for me). Possibly the tone of voice I used in responding to my husband has set a bad example for my daughter, and that is why she has a sharp tongue. Perhaps I am doing this all wrong.

I am thankful that I have learned that it is not all my fault. Part of the problem is the sin nature that our children come equipped with as they leave the womb. This very well could be most of the problem. Ecclesiastes 7:20 says, "For there is not a just man upon earth, that doeth good and sinneth not." We all struggle with the "desires of the flesh" that cause us to respond in wrong ways. Children and adults alike have relational issues throughout life that must be addressed with godly character training.

So what about the discouragement this situation can bring? Having all of your children with you all day puts a magnifying glass to these issues, and I know I have been discouraged often. But I have been discouraged before I began homeschooling. I had many letdowns when I worked full time. I have been discouraged by the actions of a friend. I have been very discouraged by strained relationships. The list of discouragements is endless. Discouragement doesn't come *because* you are homeschooling. It comes as a part of life. What you do about it will affect how well you manage during the more challenging times.

Do I humble myself and cast my cares on the Lord? Do I really believe He cares for me?

PRAYER

Heavenly Father, I confess to You that I carry too many burdens on my own shoulders. I forget to give them to You and go on. I get discouraged because I try to handle it myself. Remind me that this life is a process of growth—not an overnight success. Lift me up when it seems that my efforts are making little difference and I am feeling low. ❧

FOOD FOR THOUGHT

1. What is my greatest source of discouragement? Why? What needs to change?

2. How can I make this change successfully? List the steps in the order that they need to be taken.

3. Is there someone you know who is discouraged? How can you be an encouragement to her?

8

RAGING HORMONES

*To whom ye forgive any thing, I forgive also: for if I forgave
any thing, to whom I forgave it, for your sakes forgave I it in
the person of Christ; Lest Satan should get an advantage
of us: for we are not ignorant of his devices.*

2 CORINTHIANS 2:10-11

❧

*I*t is not uncommon for women to blame their behavior on hormones. I
have done it. Our behavior is affected by our hormonal state, and we do
well to accept this fact. Our husbands have known this to be true for a long
time. Certain times of the month, pregnancy, and menopause are all factors
that affect how we behave throughout our school day.

I remember one day last year when hormones played a role in something I did at lunch that was horrible. I was in mid-pregnancy and did not
realize that I was having a hormone level problem. I don't remember anything
going wrong in the morning, and I believe that as we sat down to lunch, nothing was out of the ordinary. I had made split pea soup, and my husband was
serving it into the bowls. My full bowl was in front of me, and my husband
did something that got under my skin. Whatever he did was really not that
great a problem, but, boy, did I react. With no warning at all I picked up the
bowl and flung it against the kitchen wall. Stunned, my family watched in
disbelief.

My reaction was totally unreasonable in light of what provoked me, and
I had no explanation for my behavior. I was unhappy to notice while clean-

ing up that the bowl had landed in my blender and broke it. As of yet, I have not made split pea soup again.

It would have been easy to blame my behavior solely on hormones. They were a factor. But the major problem was sin. I had sinned in front of the entire family. A couple of the little ones were crying, and the rest couldn't believe it. I was devastated. How could I have behaved that way? I swallowed my pride and came before my family to ask their forgiveness a little while after the incident.

This unfortunate situation became a teaching tool about sin and forgiveness. Had I let this go, my irritation with my husband would have been fueled, and I would have given Satan a foothold. Once Satan gains a foothold, all kinds of problems follow. I was grateful that I made the right choice.

Do I choose to blame hormones for my bad behavior? Is God fooled when I do this?

PRAYER

Father, forgive my childish behavior. Help me to recognize the signs that hormones are affecting me. Please show me how to detach from a situation before my behavior becomes sin. Let those who live with me be sensitive to the times when I am not feeling like myself. ❧

FOOD FOR THOUGHT

1. Have you behaved badly during a "hormone day" and failed to ask forgiveness from those you hurt in the process? Do so now.

2. Have you discovered any ways to ease the effects of raging hormones, such as exercise, progesterone cream, etc.? Consult a health practitioner and/or read some good material on the subject.

3. What are some ways you can show sensitivity to your daughter's emotional state during her "hormone days"?

9

I HOMESCHOOL

But he giveth more grace. Wherefore he saith, God resisteth
the proud, but giveth grace unto the humble.

JAMES 4:6

When I first began homeschooling, I wanted to tell everyone what we were doing. I was so excited and proud of our decision. I didn't mean to come across as thinking what I was doing was better than what others had chosen, but that is exactly what happened. Naturally when you share the news with those who are not homeschooling, there is tension as they have to process the fact that they have chosen another alternative and may begin to wonder if what they are doing is right. If you verbalize to them that you feel homeschooling is the best way to educate children, then you have created even greater tension.

Homeschooling isn't for every family. People should not be made to feel bad because they can't or don't want to homeschool. It is only by the grace of God that *I* can do it. When we boast (unfortunately this is how we sound) of our homeschooling, we fail to acknowledge the grace God has given us. We act as though we are better than others who are not homeschooling. This prideful and haughty spirit does a lot of damage in very little time.

If we show grace (goodwill or kindness) to others instead, we are likely to draw others toward us rather than repel them. As excited as we are about homeschooling, it doesn't hurt to keep quiet about it. When people learn that you are homeschooling, they will ask questions. This is a better forum to share what you are doing. Be sure to ask questions about what they are doing with their own children. Showing interest in their choices paves the way to have a friendly conversation even though you are not both homeschooling.

Ultimately we are all responsible as parents for the training of our children. Some of us delegate more of this responsibility than others, but we as parents are still responsible. How much better it is to support and encourage each other in our parental duties than to shun each other because we aren't doing it the same way. Others may approach you with a prideful spirit because they feel their educational choice is the only right one. Respond to them kindly and reflect God's grace through your response to them. Remember, in the end, it is only pleasing God that will matter. Our own behavior must always take this into account.

Do I run people over as I tell them all about homeschooling? Have I considered that everyone does not share my enthusiasm?

PRAYER

Dear Jesus, forgive the prideful, haughty spirit that developed in me as I began our homeschooling journey. Show me how to share my excitement about homeschooling with others in a humble way. Please make me more sensitive to the needs of others who may want to homeschool and can't at this time. Let me be their friend and not their enemy. ❧

FOOD FOR THOUGHT

1. Have you offended someone in your zealous approach to sharing your own views on homeschooling? Humbly apologize to this person(s) as soon as possible.

2. Think of someone who really understands your passion for homeschooling. Restrict yourself to talking to this person when you need to share your excitement about what you are doing.

1 0

RETIREMENT BENEFITS

Train up a child in the way he should go:
and when he is old, he will not depart from it.

PROVERBS 22:6

If it is the Lord's will for our seventh child to be our last, and we homeschool her through high school, we will have been homeschooling for about twenty-five years. After this "career," the benefits will be in the children and the generations to follow. When I am done homeschooling my youngest child, I will still be available to train my grandchildren. I'm not sure that a homeschooling mom ever actually retires. More likely her job description will change a bit, but she will still be very much needed.

Training our children takes a long time. Often the benefits of training our own are not readily visible. Sometimes we don't see the full impact of our efforts until they leave our home. Right up until this time we are continuing to train them up in the way they should go. We don't expect our children to leave home at age eighteen. They can live with us until they marry or have some other reason to move out. This career of homeschooling will be a long one for us.

I have observed a number of people in their retirement years who seem lost. Because so much of who they are was wrapped up in their career, they are less than complete without it. Our career as homeschooling moms will never end. Our children are our career and will not stop being our children just because we finish homeschooling them. As I anticipate my "retirement" from homeschooling, I am hoping for a second chance.

As a first-generation homeschool mom, I have much to learn. I haven't played the learning games and read to my children as often as I would have liked. When my grandchildren visit, I will have the opportunity to do some of these things with them. To me, retirement seems like a benefit in itself, when I think about how I will continue to use the skills and wisdom I have gained training my own children at home.

How do you see your role as a homeschooling mom changing as your children grow up and begin their own lives? Does this get you excited?

PRAYER

Lord, forgive me for living life only in the here and now. I get so caught up in the demands of the moment that I fail to see the blessings these efforts will bring. Keep me mindful that You have only loaned me these children for a short time. Help me to be an effective teacher while they are in my care. I pray that the "retirement" years will be an opportunity for me to be a help to my children. ❧

FOOD FOR THOUGHT

1. When all of your children have finished their formal studies, what will be the benefits to you from training them at home? Make a list of these in one column. In the next column list the benefits to your children. Praise God for all of these.

2. Do you ever wish that you had a different "career"? Would the retirement benefits be as good as in your current situation?

3. Take time to think about what a homeschooling grandmother will look like. Ask your children to tell you what they think they would want you to do as a homeschooling grandmother.

1 1

I WANT TO BE NORMAL

*Attend unto my cry; for I am brought very low: deliver me
from my persecutors; for they are stronger than I.*

PSALM 142:6

＄ome people thrive on being different. I prefer to blend in and not stand
out in a crowd. This isn't how it usually works though. Merely entering a
building with our family of nine draws attention. When people find out that
we homeschool, they have a tendency to put us in a category. "Oh, you homeschool! We thought so." I hope this is a compliment, but sometimes I'm not
so sure.

Once after we had been attending a church for a few months, I was
speaking to the pastor, and he made a comment that I wasn't expecting. He
told me that homeschoolers spend too much time with their families.
Apparently we had a different approach to family life than the members of this
church. We were just different.

It wouldn't be so bad if people could just let us be different. There are
times when being different from what is considered normal (sending your
children to school) causes problems. Some people are downright nasty about
it. After a while this can become pretty disconcerting. I have been brought low
more than once by the attacks made on us because we homeschool. It would
be easy to respond with a smart remark during these times, but there is a
better way.

It is critical to remember that God's plan for *your* family is unique to
you. Don't compare yourself to everyone that you meet. God never intended

for all of us to look alike and live exactly the same way. God created you to do specific things in this earthly life. One of them is homeschooling. Even if this isn't the "normal" approach as culture defines education, it is normal for you. Be encouraged that many others are educating their children at home even if you don't live near anyone who homeschools. Enjoy the work that the Lord has called you to do.

Are you afraid that people will label you as being different? Do you see that homeschooling is normal for you?

PRAYER

Dear Lord, help those who observe our family to be accepting of our decision to homeschool. May their criticism of this choice be silenced. I pray for those who would persecute us for our decision. Let them respect us for following Your call on our own unique family. Please prompt me to be accepting of those who have chosen a different educational track than I have. Let me not forget that You have a special plan for each family. ❧

FOOD FOR THOUGHT

1. Is the fear of what others may think of homeschooling holding you back from getting started or continuing what you have already begun? Does criticism undermine your confidence in your decision to homeschool?

2. Do you know how to respond appropriately when someone attacks you because you homeschool? Discuss this with your husband (or pastor if you are a single mom).

3. Explain why you have decided to homeschool to your children. Particularly if you have taken them out of public or private schools, make sure that they understand that educating at home is just as normal as other options available. Be sure that they don't feel odd or superior because of your decision. Strike this delicate balance.

1 2

HOW MUCH DOES THIS COST?

*Then said Jesus unto his disciples, If any man will come after me,
let him deny himself, and take up his cross, and follow me.*

MATTHEW 16:24

❧

Discipleship costs us something. Jesus made it clear that self-denial is a part
of the program. While on the surface it seems rather obvious that as homeschooling moms we have to give up a few things, it goes much deeper than
that. Homeschooling becomes a lifestyle that will not allow you to do some
of the things you used to do, but opens the door for new opportunities at
the same time.

I enjoyed a weekly Bible study when the children were all young. I was
involved in a MOPs group for nearly nine years. Before my children were
born, I participated in a junior women's club. Homeschooling has limited
the time I have for these activities. My interests have also changed. Fellowship
with other homeschoolers is more important to me now. I still continue
with Bible study, but it is done on my own instead of with a group.

In following Jesus we are asked to deny ourselves. That means that we
will have to say no to some good things. My husband had a part-time job in
a church where he was in charge of maintenance. He brought our young
sons with him to work. The boys were helpful and learned skills from their
dad while they worked. This arrangement was a good one for some time.
Church workers smiled as the boys brought their tool boxes into the building. They were only four and six, but they worked hard. One day a new pastor came to the church and outlawed the practice of children working

alongside their parents. My husband quit the job because training his boys was more important.

Sometimes what we have to give up when we are homeschooling isn't so obvious at the beginning. Friendships often change. Schedules with other families who do not homeschool don't always coordinate very well. If you homeschool through the summer, this makes it even more challenging. A few close friends who also homeschool are about all I have time for right now. This is something I have had to accept as part of denying myself at this time.

I see homeschooling as a calling from the Lord to minister to my family in a particular way. This calling is specifically for right now. It precludes many other things that I could be doing with my time. Hobbies and free time are almost history as I struggle to carve out a little time. This is okay, because in doing what the Lord wants me to do, I am willing to pay the price.

Did you count the cost before you began homeschooling? Is it more than you expected?

PRAYER

Dear Father, I thank You for sending Your Son, Jesus, to earth to pay the penalty for my sins. This was a great price to pay. Help me to cheerfully count the cost of our homeschooling decision. Encourage me when my flesh does not want to deny self. Make me more like Jesus.

FOOD FOR THOUGHT

1. What have I given up as a homeschool mom? Has it been worth it?
2. As I have given up some things, what have I gained in the process?
3. Praise God for allowing you such an opportunity to deny self.

13

WE ARE ALL DONE

For this cause shall a man leave his father and mother, and shall be
joined unto his wife, and they two shall be one flesh.

EPHESIANS 5:31

My oldest child is a young teenager. It feels as if I will be homeschooling forever. In reality, it will be over in the blink of an eye. While our children are always with us, it is ironic to realize that we are preparing them to leave.

Our family attended the wedding of one of my husband's coworkers. The bride and groom had both been living at home with their parents until they were married. As I watched them at the altar, I could see that this young woman was being released from the protection of her father to the protection of her husband. It gave me a vision for my own children as they grow up and marry. The training that we are doing now is preparation for them to leave our home and have productive lives of their own.

I am already preparing them for this time by helping them to develop a vision. We talk about what they might want to do after the completion of their formal studies. The girls have interests such as flower-arranging, gardening, and sewing. The boys will have many options with their handyman father. I, too, must prepare for the day when they will leave our home. During the busiest of moments I think about my role as a grandmother.

A time will come when homeschooling will be officially complete. Your children will move on with the rest of their lives. One of our goals as homeschool moms should be to give them the best preparation possible for their future. It is never too early to begin talking about what they might like to do as adults. Spend hours at this over the years. Help them develop a vision for what God has intended for them. Assist them in getting ready to leave when the time comes.

Do I remember that someday my children will be gone, or do I have tunnel vision as I work to get through today's lesson? Do I need to look more at the bigger picture?

PRAYER

Lord, help me to be ready for the day when my children leave home. I know they will not be at home with me forever, but while I have them, show me Your will for each of them so that I can prepare each one as best I can. Give me the strength to see this work to its end successfully. ❧

FOOD FOR THOUGHT

1. Have you thought about what your child will do after formal home-schooling is complete? Consider this as you teach them now.
2. Take some time to evaluate each of your children. What are their strengths and weaknesses? What are their temperaments? What are their interests? Compile this information and sit down with each one to go over it.
3. Develop a vision with your child for the future. Set up a tentative plan that you are working toward. Set up objectives to meet in order to successfully attain this goal. (Example: If your daughter wants to be a good wife and mother, then she needs to be prepared to cook, clean, etc.) Modify your plan as God reveals what He wants each of your children to do.

1 4

HELP! WHAT DO I DO NOW?

If any of you lack wisdom, let him ask of God, that giveth to
all men liberally, and upbraideth not; and it shall be given him.

JAMES 1:5

Whenever one of my children ends up with the stomach flu, I hope in the back of my mind that only that child will get sick. A couple of times this was the case. But most often it passes through the family. For a large family, this can be quite an experience. I remember one time when *all* of us got sick.

My fifth child, Joanna, was only a couple of months old. I got sick first while my husband was away. He came home three hours later, and a couple of the other children were already sick. I was very weak, and all I could do was lie in bed. One of the older children brought Joanna to my room to nurse and took her away when she was done. Hour by hour as I listened to the rest of the family get sick, I felt helpless as I was too weak to be of any assistance. My husband took over and did well until he got the flu bug—the last to succumb. Our family was a sorry sight for the next twenty-four hours.

Compared to a death in the family, loss of a job, and a host of other disruptions, our family flu seems mild. It did, however, qualify as a crisis for our family. It required drastic modification to our schedule for a couple of days. What you consider a crisis may be different from someone else's crisis. Some people handle certain situations better than others. Some problems may seem like a crisis, but they are just part of a normal day. Two sentences ago I ran to the basement to address an overflowing laundry tub (just a minor inconvenience).

In times of crisis it is important to take swift and decisive action. Modify your school schedule to minimize stress and then get back on track as soon as possible. Seek the Lord's wisdom in understanding why you are facing the trial. This will help you to respond more appropriately to it. Rejoice in knowing that character growth is a part of the process of pressing on through the trial. Remember your school plans, but hold on to them loosely until the crisis has passed and you can resume.

Is there a crisis in your life requiring you to modify your plans? Make those changes now.

PRAYER

Heavenly Father, make me sensitive to those times where I need to change my plans. Help me to recognize a crisis for what it is and take the necessary steps to deal with it effectively. Grant me wisdom to understand what You want me to learn through this process. Help me to accept the situation for what it is and turn to You for direction. ❧

FOOD FOR THOUGHT

1. Has a circumstance in your life become a trial for you? Why would God allow this trial to happen in *your* life?
2. What do you think God would have you learn through this experience?
3. Make a list of all of the women you know who are experiencing a crisis right now. How can you minister to their emotional needs during this time? Helping others will help you get through your own time of trial.

1 5

DAILY EMOTIONS

Observe and hear all these words which I command thee,
that it may go well with thee, and with thy children after thee
for ever, when thou doest that which is good and right
in the sight of the Lord thy God

DEUTERONOMY 12:28

🌿

I have on a number of occasions felt as if I was not in my "right mind." The cause of this condition is varied—pregnancy, stress, overload, etc. The result is the same. I can't evaluate circumstances properly because my emotions are clouding my thinking. I know, it is hard for a woman to admit, but it is true: We tend to be more emotional than men, and therefore our judgment is sometimes clouded when our emotions get out of control.

I am having this problem now as I am in the middle of writing this book, moving to a farm, nursing an infant, training a two-year-old, home-schooling, etc. This is too much for me, and stress is steering my emotional state into the danger zone. My husband can confirm that I have totally lost perspective and am overreacting to too many things. My children understand this problem, too. They are spending the entire day with me and have no means of escape.

I cannot lighten my load right at this moment. In a month or two it will change, but for now I need to commit to respond appropriately to circumstances regardless of how I feel. Wow! This seems impossible. When I reread Deuteronomy 12:28, it seems imperative. To respond correctly to a situation when you feel totally the opposite is superhuman. It is in fact divine. It is by God's grace that we are able to do the right thing at the right time.

I confess that I don't recognize that my emotions are slipping soon enough. If I did, I would decide in my mind how to proceed and would pay little heed to my emotional response. I would choose to apply biblical principles even if I did not feel like doing so. I would save myself many headaches from the relationship repair that must be done after emotional slip-ups. This is much easier said than done, but seeking the Lord's direction during these times can completely change the outcome. We cannot figure this out on our own while in the middle of an emotional fog.

Is something tipping your emotional scale so far out of balance that you need some help? You are not alone. I need help, too.

PRAYER

Father, I am in such a state today. I have let my emotions get the best of me again. Emotions are good, but sometimes I just feel too much. Help me to balance it all again and make decisions rationally. Don't let me sink any further, but help me to get right back up to where I should be. Forgive the sins I have committed with my mouth while I allowed my emotions to control me. ❧

FOOD FOR THOUGHT

1. Is there a situation that is seemingly too much for you to handle? How are you responding emotionally?
2. How are the emotions of your children today? Of your husband? Help them where you can.
3. Take time to understand the difference between the mind, the will, and the emotions. Remember that the emotions should never be "in charge" of your life.

16

GO, SISTER, GO

And of some have compassion, making a difference.

JUDE 22

❧

*I*t sure helps to have cheerleaders. Sports teams have them because it helps the players to do a better job on the field when they know others are behind them cheering them on. Employees thrive when they receive the praise of their boss. Children do well when their parents praise them often. Homeschool moms need encouragement, too. Sometimes that encouragement is essential for them to continue.

We *all* need encouragement. Challenges come and we feel burdened. We get tired and sometimes lose interest. We are unsure of ourselves or our children. But there are times when we just need someone to cheer us on when the going gets rough. Circumstances will sometimes make life so difficult that it is tough to keep going.

It is so important to help others who find themselves in this situation. Homeschool moms understand each other and know best what would be the most help. Our lifestyles are unique, and other people may not know how to help us. Bringing over a meal may not be enough. Taking the children for the day might be just right. This could be a time for a field trip with two families. Or maybe the two mothers could go out alone and just have some quiet time to talk.

I know a couple of women who had some tough times in their lives. I thought about what I might need during such a trial. I realized that women need to be treated as special. They give so much of themselves to their families that often there is little left for themselves. I made a point of providing little treats for them as often as I could. One week I gave them some hand lotion. Another week I gave them a taped sermon that I had found very encouraging. Little touches mean a lot to a woman who is experiencing some trying times. A phone call with a verse of Scripture to encourage can work wonders.

A compassionate heart is one that is easily moved by the distresses and sufferings of another. When you show compassion to another homeschooling mom, you are making a difference. Your practical assistance can be very valuable to a woman who is not able to carry the load by herself at that time. In bearing one another's burdens, we are serving the Lord, and this is pleasing to God.

Is there a woman that you could encourage through a difficult circumstance? How can you best meet her need?

PRAYER

Lord, make me more aware of the needs of the women around me. Help me to remember to ask them how they are doing. Show me how to be an encouragement to those in need. Teach me to have compassion for others instead of judging them. Give me a heart for people and a burden for their souls. Keep me focused on others ahead of myself. ❧

FOOD FOR THOUGHT

1. Is there a homeschooling family you know who is experiencing difficult circumstances that may not be fully understood by those unfamiliar with the demands of a homeschooling lifestyle?

2. In what ways could you come alongside the mother to ease her burden?

3. Are there women who have come alongside you in your hour of need? Write them a note of appreciation.

17

I'M SORRY

The discretion of a man deferreth his anger; and it is his glory to pass over a transgression.

PROVERBS 19:11

ॐ

I had to look up the word *transgression* to really understand this verse. It means an offense. This verse is telling me that it is my glory to overlook the times that others do something that offends (or irritates) me. Oh boy. This is a tough one. I can't say that I apply this too well yet. I really blew it with my friend last winter.

Good friends are important. Friendships grow closer when we spend time together. As homeschooling moms, we have little discretionary time, and I cherish those opportunities to get together with my friend. We had planned to get together over the winter with our husbands, too. The four of us get along quite well. I made a number of efforts to schedule something, but it never worked out. As winter was drawing to a close, I decided that my friend probably didn't really like me that much after all, and I wasn't going to make any more efforts. My husband tried to assure me that there must be some good explanation for her seeming lack of interest, but I didn't really listen to him (bad move!).

Finally in the spring my friend and I got together. Somehow we got on the subject of our inability to meet over the winter. It was interesting to find that she was feeling negative toward me because she felt that I had withdrawn from her. Ironically, there never was a big problem. We both had some struggles, and we just weren't able to see each other as often as we normally do. By being honest with each other, we were able to understand each other's circumstances and drew closer through the process. I felt accepted by her even though I had let her down.

Christ's love for us is like that. Our sin lets Him down each day, but He died on the cross of Calvary to take the punishment for our sins. He loves us in spite of the way we act. He does not withdraw from us. When we stop and take the time to tell Him we are sorry for the way we have behaved, we draw closer to Him. What a friend!

Do you have a friendship that may need some tender loving care right now? Humbly initiate a loving chat at your earliest opportunity.

PRAYER

Dear Father, thank You for Your eternal patience with me. I don't always know how to relate to others as I should. I put my own feelings and needs ahead of my friend's. Show me how to be the best friend I can be. Prompt me to free up more of my time to be a good friend. Thank You for the role model of Your Son to help me grow closer to You. ◁

FOOD FOR THOUGHT

1. Do you have a close friend who stays with you through thick and thin?

2. What have you done to keep your relationship strong when conflicts arise? Apply these same principles to other relationships.

3. Close friendships are sometimes difficult to attain in our busy lives. What can you do to be more available when you meet someone that you "click" with? Develop ways of staying close even when you are both busy.

1 8

STRATEGIES TO FIT THEIR STYLE

And he saith unto them, Follow me, and
I will make you fishers of men.

MATTHEW 4:19

I have looked at articles and heard talks about learning styles. They say it is important to identify your child's and your own learning style and tailor your methods for optimal results. While I have tried to do this, I end up forgetting which methods are best for each child. In short, I get confused. I have tried to make this easier to apply.

In its simplest form, I am observing whether my child learns best by looking at his work, hearing his work, or touching his work. Since we have all three learning styles in our home, it is still a challenge to keep my methods consistent with the needs of each child. Some time ago I decided that by including all three methods (visual, auditory, kinesthetic) of learning into our homeschool, each child would have access to his favored learning style at least some of the time. This works pretty well, but I believe Jesus exemplified the best way for us.

In Matthew 4 we see the beginning of Jesus' ministry and the calling out of the first disciples. How did He get their attention? He spoke their language. He talked in terms they could understand. Peter and Andrew were brothers who made their living as fishermen. Jesus called them by saying, "Follow me, and I will make you fishers of men" (Matt. 4:19). He spoke few words to the two men, but the words He used were powerful and easy for Peter and Andrew to understand.

Sometimes we make the lesson too difficult for our children to understand because we complicate the teaching methods. Learn to speak the language your children know. If your son likes soccer, then learn all you can about the game and teach him using soccer terminology as often as possible. If your daughter loves to cook, the kitchen offers many good teaching opportunities.

My husband is a firefighter, and there are times when he doesn't understand me. If I try again to communicate my thoughts using fire terminology, we usually have a good laugh as he understands exactly what I meant the first time. The same is true for me. When points are illustrated in terms of what I experience in my home as a homemaker and mother, I catch on pretty quickly.

Do you and your child speak the same language? Do you need to learn more about his favorite things?

PRAYER

Lord, thank You for giving me such good examples of teaching through Your parables. You touched the lives of many because You spoke to them in their own language. Help me to be more sensitive to the way my child learns. Remind me to use his favorite things to illustrate my points often. Let Your teaching style become my own so that I can be more effective in the teaching of my child. ❧

FOOD FOR THOUGHT

1. Make a list of each of your children's favorite topics. (It could be cats, trains, inline skating, reading, etc.). Try to think of ways to use this interest of theirs to help illustrate their lessons in all subject areas.
2. Practice being aware of these topics on the list.
3. Rejoice every time you can make something more clear to your child using this method.

1 9

THE CONSTANCY OF IT ALL

*The woman saith unto him, Sir, thou hast nothing to draw with, and
the well is deep: from whence then hast thou that living water?*

JOHN 4:11

I was sitting in a chair one afternoon with my feet up when I realized that
for every minute that passed, I had three questions being asked of me. After
a while I felt as if I was going into mental shutdown. My husband was at
work (overnight at the fire station), and by 5:45 P.M. I had decided to take a
fifteen-minute break in my bedroom. This kept me from being impatient with
the children, allowed me a chance to take a deep breath, and gave me the
energy to get them ready for bed.

While the constancy of all the questions was exhausting to me, I did
notice that as a homeschooling mom, my influence *is* constant. That is one
of the reasons we homeschool. This is a true blessing if we can learn to manage the sensory overload homeschooling brings our way. While successful
business executives can give us some clues, there is someone else who is the
perfect model for us.

Jesus met the needs of many, many people. Not only did He speak to the
masses, but He met with people individually. When He met the woman at
the well, He was there to quench His thirst. Even then He met up with someone who had a need that He could meet. He did not turn her away, but
took the opportunity to teach the woman of her need for a Savior. Jesus
took the time to answer the many questions that were asked of Him. We
should, too!

Jesus was personal and patient with people. He listened to them. He answered them. He did the work of His Father. I feel responsible to cover the subjects that are taught in the public schools. I take time to make sure my curriculum and my schedule meet this state requirement. I *should* make sure that my schedule has daily unstructured time for my children to ask me questions. One of the reasons that I am bombarded by questions all throughout the day is that the children know this is the only way to get their needs addressed. By not making myself more accessible to them, I have encouraged them to ask me things whenever they can get a word in edgewise.

Do I give my children a chance just to talk to me? Do my children know that their questions are important to me?

PRAYER

Father, thank You for sending Your Son, Jesus, to show me how to relate to people in need. My children need me, and I confess that I don't always know how to meet their needs. I don't always take the time to meet the needs I know how to meet. I get overwhelmed with the constant demands put upon me, and I end up crabby. Renew me, Lord, and make me personal and patient with my children.

FOOD FOR THOUGHT

1. What aspect of your homeschooling lifestyle seems to be a constant drain on you? What can you do to change this? (Example—change your attitude, circumstances, etc.)

2. When Jesus was surrounded by people constantly, He got alone to pray. Do you get alone to pray regularly?

3. Create a place in your home to pray. It can even be a closet!

2 0

No, I Can't Do That Right Now

*And he said unto them, When ye pray, say, Our Father
which art in heaven, Hallowed be thy name. Thy kingdom come.
Thy will be done, as in heaven, so in earth.*

LUKE 11:2

I couldn't decide whether or not to take the soul-winning course at our church. I knew that one of my weak areas was sharing the Gospel clearly with others, so I signed up. The class was demanding, meeting once a week for fourteen weeks. We had homework and memorized over twenty verses. It began in the spring and finished near the end of June—exactly one month after the birth of our seventh child. Several times during the class I doubted whether I should have taken it. Just three days after the birth of my baby, I was at church sitting in class because I knew if I missed two classes in a row, I would never finish. I did finish, but just barely.

It isn't always easy to say no to outside commitments. Many good opportunities are beckoning us. After saying no so often, sometimes we feel guilty and reluctantly give in and sign up for something we really can't handle. Our time as homeschool moms is pretty much filled already. For some reason, people expect us to have more time when in reality we have less.

It becomes even more important for us to choose outside obligations that support our family goals. One of the reasons that I went ahead and took the soul-winning course is for the purpose of becoming equipped to train our children to share the Gospel clearly. This goal was compatible with our family goals and made it well worth the extra effort it took to finish the course.

People will always have opinions about how you should spend your time. Don't let the expectations of others run *your* household. Seek the Lord's will about what your family should do rather than listening to the opinions of other people. "Thy will be done." Input from other people is fine, but ultimately it is the Lord Jesus Christ you are pleasing.

Do you suffer from guilt when you tell someone that you cannot do what he or she asks? Does this tendency push you to overcommit yourself?

PRAYER

Heavenly Father, thank You for giving me so many wonderful ways to spend my time. Help me to narrow my choices to those options that fit with the direction You are taking my family. Give me the courage to say no to things that are not a good fit right now. Grant me wisdom to stretch myself when the right opportunities present themselves. Make me so sensitive to Your will for me that I regularly make good decisions about how to spend my time. ✑

FOOD FOR THOUGHT

1. Are you overcommitted? Can you get out of some things so that you keep only those activities that are God's will for you? Pray about how to make this happen.

2. How can you prevent overcommitment from happening in the future? Could your husband or prayer partner hold you accountable?

3. What can you do to teach your children about choosing outside activities wisely? Could you make goals with your children regarding this area and then help them to see God's best for them?

2 1

EDUCATION IS A CHOICE

If any man teach otherwise, and consent not to wholesome words,
even the words of our Lord Jesus Christ, and to the doctrine which
is according to godliness; He is proud, knowing nothing, but
doting about questions and strifes of words, whereof
cometh envy, strife, railings, evil surmisings.

1   T I M O T H Y   6 : 3 - 4

❦

A Christian college in our area sponsored a debate on the topic of whether or not Christians should take their children out of public schools. The topic grieved me. The question should not even have been asked. I anticipated a division among the Christians who attended the debate, and my fears were confirmed by the many letters to the editor of our local newspaper for weeks.

We can divide into factions with our attitudes. While our family believes it is God's best to homeschool our children, that belief is for our own family. I cannot decide for other families what God's best is for them. There is no reason why I should not respect their decisions to educate their children differently. Our pastor explained this to me in a way that really makes sense.

He said that parents are responsible for the education of their children. Some parents delegate more of this than others. It is as simple as that. When we have our children sit with us in church to hear the sermon, we are delegating some of our responsibility to the pastor. When we take our children to music lessons, we are delegating some of our responsibility to the music teacher. Parents with children in private or public schools have chosen to delegate more than homeschool parents, but as parents we are all responsible for the education of our children.

Homeschool, private, and public school parents need to stop bashing one another. We must stop quarreling over educational choice. If we major on the majors (building good, godly relationships) and take our focus off of the minors (which educational method we have chosen), I believe that Christ will have much greater opportunity to work in us and through us.

Do you look down on others who have not chosen to homeschool their children? Is pride a problem here?

PRAYER

Dear Lord, please forgive me for any attitudes that I have had regarding how other people should educate their children. In my enthusiasm about our home-schooling, I'm sure I have hurt some feelings. Keep me ever mindful that You have not desired for all of us to look the same and do everything exactly the same way. Thank You for our homeschooling experience. Let that not be a stumbling block to a friendship with a family who does not homeschool. ⊰

FOOD FOR THOUGHT

1. Have you in any way offended someone else because you homeschool and they don't? Make a list of possible offenses and make them right if possible.
2. What is your attitude toward homeschooling? Do you feel it is the best and only way to train children? What effect does this attitude have on others who do not homeschool?
3. Take a piece of paper. Divide it into three columns. Head them with "home-school," "private school," and "public school." Write down the pros and cons of each educational choice. Then think of people you know who do not homeschool. Meditate on the benefits of the educational choice they have made. Praise God that all of us have the responsibility for our own choices.

2 2

SUCH A SACRIFICE

*And he said to them all, If any man will come after me, let him
deny himself, and take up his cross daily, and follow me.*

LUKE 9:23

𝒫eople have made comments to me that indicate they think that I have
given up my whole life to homeschool my children. In some ways I have,
but that is not entirely true. I am reminded of the guard bees in the beehive.
It is their job to protect the hive. Once they sting an intruder, they will soon
die. I don't have it nearly so bad.

Probably the most striking sacrifice I have to make is to give up my personal time. I observe women taking classes, joining clubs, going out shopping, and I wonder where such time would fit in my life. A number of years
ago I took a volleyball class at the park district so that I would get some
exercise and have something that I liked to do. Before I had children, I took
a class on wood refinishing and refinished my bedside table. I just don't
have time for these activities anymore.

While I miss the freedom to do what I want to do, I'm not sure that it is
homeschooling that restricts my freedom the most. When Jesus talks about
the cost of discipleship, He says that we must deny ourselves and take up
our cross daily. For the homeschooling mom, this means giving up personal
time. For other mothers to "deny self" will mean something else. For all of
us, it means that our very walk with the Lord is affected by how we view the
cost of discipleship.

While I have less personal time, do I really give up that much? I see that there may be more to gain than to give up when homeschooling. The relationships that I have with my children are close. The children are close to each other, too. I know what they are learning and where their weak areas are so that I can strengthen them in these areas. I am with them so much of the time that I can see how closely they are walking with the Lord. I can see when they begin to fall away. There is not really anything I can think of that I would rather do than this.

Do I crave time alone so much that I miss the blessings of being a homeschool mom? When I do take a minute for myself, do I feel guilty?

PRAYER

Heavenly Father, thank You for giving me Your Son as an example of sacrifice. He gave His life so that my sins could be forgiven and I might have eternal life. How minor my own sacrifices to homeschool my children seem. Forgive me for my selfishness in wanting to fulfill my own desires. I seek You now for direction so that I know what You desire for me. In following Your will for me, I choose to deny my own preferences for those that You deem best for me. ❧

FOOD FOR THOUGHT

1. What sacrifices have you made to homeschool your children?
2. Have you given up anything that really mattered? If so, how do you feel about that? Can you fit it back into your life if it is God's will to do so?
3. Make a list of all the blessings that you have received because you are homeschooling.

2 3

ALONE WITH THE LORD

*For the word of God is quick, and powerful, and sharper than
any two-edged sword, piercing even to the dividing asunder
of soul and spirit, and of the joints and marrow, and is a
discerner of the thoughts and intents of the heart.*

HEBREWS 4:12

❧

There are times when there is simply more to do than I can manage. I am
feeling that way today. I cannot change my circumstances, but also I cannot
do all that must be done. I keep trying, but it isn't enough. I am physically
exhausted and mentally drained. I still keep plugging on. It doesn't help too
much. Only one thing helps—opening my Bible.

The Bible is a source of strength as the Holy Spirit brings the words of
Scripture alive when we read them. The key is that we must read them. It is
very easy to get caught up in the demands of the moment and miss God's
special source of strength for us. I do this far too frequently. Even though I
know that I *need* to have a regular quiet time every day, I still haven't made
this happen. I do well for a few weeks, and then something upsets the schedule, and I get off track again. Failure is guaranteed as I cut off the power of
the Holy Spirit to help me when I don't read my Bible daily.

The solutions to all of our problems are found in Scripture. My relationship with Jesus is built upon the Word of God. All the goodness found
in the Bible is a balm for the weary soul—an oasis for the thirsty homeschool mom who feels she is alone on the desert. Why, then, don't we make

it a priority as we do our math lessons? Why isn't our time alone with God more precious than anything else we do?

Satan does not want us to have God's power behind our homeschooling efforts. Have you ever noticed that while much of what you are trying to do with your children is going well, your devotional time is tough to keep consistent? Our devotional time, our time alone with the Lord, is the most important preparation that we have. When we faithfully read our Bible and fellowship with the Lord, it becomes more difficult for Satan to gain ground in our life. Our children are motivated by our good example to be faithful in their devotional life. Only good can come of a regular daily devotional time.

Am I faithful in my daily devotions? Are my children?

PRAYER

Father, forgive me for neglecting the most important part of my life—my devotional life. I have made excuses for not taking time each day to be alone with You. I have allowed Satan an open door into our family. Help me to take this much more seriously and show me how best to be faithful to follow through each day. Teach me to overcome the obstacles and do it right. ⋙

FOOD FOR THOUGHT

1. Make a list of all that prevents you from faithfully having daily personal devotions. Eliminate all of these distractions if you can.

2. Have a friend hold you accountable for your daily devotional time.

3. Include Scripture memory in your daily devotional life.

2 4

WHAT ABOUT PREPARATION TIME?

Be careful for nothing; but in every thing by prayer and supplication with thanksgiving let your requests be made known unto God.

PHILIPPIANS 4:6

I strongly dislike getting ready for vacation. Packing clothing for nine people, menu plans, camping gear, and all the rest gets to be too much. While I am packing, I inevitably begin to feel as though I do not really want to go on vacation after all. "It is too much work. It isn't worth it. Let's just stay home." Once we are packed and on our way, we usually have a good time. I just barely make it through the preparation stage though.

School preparation is another one of those necessary steps to something worthwhile. I rarely have enough time to plan and get ready for a new school year. While I used to enjoy lining up all the books and figuring out our schedule, it has become more tedious with so many children. I desire to have a well-laid-out plan for the entire year, but usually end up with a simple outline instead.

The obstacles to overcome to get that precious quiet time for school preparation are amazing. Our family does a skit when I speak to home-school groups. In the skit I am trying to get through a box of curriculum and barely get started because of all the interruptions. The skit ends with my husband bringing in the baby with a nasty diaper that needs attention now! "Oh well, I guess I will look at these books a little later."

And so it goes. More often than not, I don't have the time I believe I need to prepare our lessons. I wonder if the time just doesn't happen because

I really don't need to prepare the schoolwork as much as I need to prepare in other areas. In Paul's letter to the Philippians, he is telling them not to be anxious, but to pray and ask God for what they need. When I do that, it seems that God provides in ways that are different from what I was expecting.

The best preparation for the school year is to do my best to prepare the lessons and make certain that I prepare my heart. Has your school time ever gone well even when you couldn't spend the time preparing as you had hoped? Why is that? I believe that when you seek the Lord's wisdom in your time of need, He gives you just exactly what you need, whether you realize it or not.

PRAYER

Dear Lord, thank You for allowing me access to You at all hours of the day and night. I need not worry about anything because I can bring it to You in prayer instead. Forgive me for having shortsighted plans for our school year that mostly consist of lesson plans and curriculum. More importantly, prepare my heart to train my children properly to bring glory and honor to You. ❦

FOOD FOR THOUGHT

1. Consider the advantages of putting together an outline that can be changed over the school year, as opposed to rigid plans that are a lot of work to alter when the unexpected comes up.

2. Involve your children in the planning process. Teach them how to organize their time and work efficiently.

3. Begin thinking about next year early enough so that you can get all of your materials in plenty of time.

2 5

WHAT'S SO FUNNY?

A time to weep, and a time to laugh;
a time to mourn, and a time to dance.

ECCLESIASTES 3:4

❧

When Jimmy was three years old, he did something very funny. I am so glad that I saw it that way from the beginning. Our home, although small, was on four levels. The top level had a master bedroom and bath. When a child went up there, and everyone else was on the main floor, it was hard to tell what he or she was up to. Jimmy had gone upstairs, and when I went to check on him, I found my son with his father's shaving cream. He had very artistically arranged the foam all over the wallpapered wall. It was a humorous sight even though it did discolor the wallpaper.

Usually this would send me into a training mode where I would have discussed everything from disobedience to the price of new wallpaper. Instead I chuckled and got the rest of the family to see Jimmy's project. I felt a little guilty because our art classes were a bit weak. Jimmy knew he was wrong, and he didn't do it again. We eventually took down the wallpaper and painted the wall.

The reason I handled this well was because I took the time to laugh. The damage was done, and all I could do was clean up anyway. Getting irritated about the whole thing wouldn't have helped.

A sense of humor is just what a homeschool mom needs. I find it easy to weep, but why do I forget to laugh? Many times each day the children do things that (if I had a better sense of humor) should make me laugh.

Take Jimmy, for example. Now that he is a little older, he is getting into bigger trouble than the shaving cream episode. When he was five years old, he pulled the fire alarm at church in the afternoon. His firefighter dad wasn't too pleased. I found it humorous. Jimmy was told by the lieutenant that his actions were wrong, and our son said he was sorry. When he was seven, he was found in our neighbor's tree trimming branches with a saw. I am glad that I was able to see the humor in it.

Does it drive you crazy when your children get into things? Have they done some funny things that you forgot to laugh about because you got irritated instead?

PRAYER

Lord, make me a mom with a sense of humor. Take away my prim and proper approach to everything and let me relax and enjoy the children more. Show me the funny side of life since I so easily take it too seriously. Help me to show my children how to laugh at themselves and learn to be less overcome by their failures. I have much to learn and so much time for my children to teach me with their antics. Keep me aware of when it is time to laugh. ⋙

FOOD FOR THOUGHT

1. When was the last time you saw the humor in a situation, and it helped you to handle it better? Reflect on the outcome of the situation.
2. Commit to lighten up enough to see the humor in the everyday happenings in your home.
3. Model a sense of humor for your children. Laugh at yourself once in a while. Laugh together often.

2 6

WHERE'S DAD?

*And he shall turn the heart of the fathers to the children, and
the heart of the children to their fathers, lest I come
and smite the earth with a curse.*

MALACHI 4:6

⁓

This verse is a real eye-opener for me. It doesn't say anywhere that it is the wife who turns the father's heart toward the children. No wonder my efforts did not work. The role of the father in the homeschool is not defined by the wife; it is defined by the Lord. This can be a little trying for the wife who doesn't understand what the Lord is saying to her husband. It becomes more confusing if the husband isn't listening to the Lord.

Most homeschool moms that I know are pretty much responsible for everything involved in their decision to homeschool. Few dads are actively involved in homeschooling. That is the way it seems anyway. I used to think that Dad should teach a few subjects, give me time to plan lessons, help look over the schoolwork, and more. The only problem is that he works a full-time job. It is not really a problem, but desirable that he work. I did not initially understand what Dad's role should be.

I can't tell Dad his role. He has to develop it himself. Tell him of your needs, but don't present a step-by-step plan to meet them. Let him lead. Seek his guidance. Value his input. Cherish his help. Show your appreciation for the responsibility God has given *him* as the head of your family.

As homeschool moms we tend to expect that our husbands will do exactly what we need them to do so that we can be successful. It doesn't always work that way. We must learn to work with what we have and make the best of it. It takes time for dads to understand just how they fit into the homeschool. Smart moms give them time to figure this out.

Does your husband meet all of your expectations regarding his involvement in your school? Give your expectations to God and let your husband fill his role as God calls him.

PRAYER

Thank You, Lord, that my husband takes an active role in the training of our children. I am grateful for his involvement. Forgive me for wanting him to do so much more. The load I carry is great, and I forget that he has many other responsibilities in his life, too. Help me to seek his advice more often than I complain to him. Gently prod me to try his ideas even when they make no sense to me. Keep me mindful of my role as the mother, and let me allow my husband the room to develop his role as the father. Thank You for calling my husband's heart to his children. ❧

FOOD FOR THOUGHT

1. Do you communicate your needs to your husband and then allow him to meet them? Do you accept his answers to your concerns?
2. Study 1 Peter 3 and meditate on your role as a wife. Ask your husband to tell you how well you are following these verses. Commit to working on your weak areas.
3. Praise God for the time that your husband devotes to your family.

2 7

WHY DOESN'T SHE HELP?

*Grudge not one against another, brethren, lest ye be condemned:
behold, the judge standeth before the door.*

JAMES 5:9

❧

I feel bad when people misunderstand me. Sometimes I don't even know about it. Someone has an attitude toward me or just steers clear of my path. It is really hard to take at church. It happens with the women. In churches that are heavily involved in activities where families are separated from one another this problem crops up often.

I am thankful that my church is so family-minded. Whole family activities are common. I haven't always had this experience. Some churches we have attended had few activities for the entire family. I had to choose my areas of involvement wisely to coordinate with our homeschooling. Some women did not understand why I could not participate in some things.

It is difficult for homeschooling moms to be as involved as other women in the women's activities of the church. The demands of homeschooling are great but give us many more opportunities for ministry with our children. I have chosen to include my daughters as we minister to women through our home business, and this eliminates some of the time I might spend in church activities. While this is a wonderful fit for our family, others have misunderstood my lack of involvement at church as lack of commitment.

I also have the added challenge of my husband's work hours. He works a twenty-four-hour shift every third day, which means there will always be times when I will have to miss a class or a meeting. Even putting me on the nursery schedule is complicated because when I am the only adult (on Sundays that my husband works), it is necessary for me to be with my children. People don't always understand why I can't do something, but I am grateful for those who accept it without criticizing me.

Do you have an attitude toward any women at your church because they don't help where you think they should? Confess this judgmental spirit and then ask them if you can help them in some way.

PRAYER

Father, help me to remember that I don't usually know all of the facts about anything. It is not my position to evaluate the commitments of other women. Create in me a compassionate heart that yearns to help others who may be overwhelmed, rather than criticizing them for lack of involvement. Help me to select my church activities wisely and include my children where it is Your will to do so. Thank You for allowing me to do some things by myself, too. Please guide me as to what these commitments should be. Help me never to judge another woman because she has chosen to spend her time differently from me. ✎

FOOD FOR THOUGHT

1. Reflect upon the times women have misunderstood you when you said no to activities at church. Did you respond appropriately? How could you have improved your reaction?

2. Do you use homeschooling as an excuse not to be involved in church activities? Make sure you have committed to do something at your church that fits your family schedule. If you have trouble fitting into the existing structure, consider starting something new, such as nursing home visitation that would include your children.

3. Look for ways to serve other women.

2 8

LET'S PRAY!

Confess your faults one to another, and pray one for another,
that ye may be healed. The effectual fervent prayer of
a righteous man availeth much.

JAMES 5:16

❧

$\mathcal{A}$t our house the person who prays before the meal says, "Let's pray" so that all know it is time to bow their heads and fold their hands. This practice works well as a cue for the family. I wonder why we only do this at mealtimes. Perhaps it is more of a habit to pray before meals than it is to pray at other times. We should make prayer a habit throughout our day. It is a powerful privilege to be able to pray in our homeschool, and we should embrace it warmly.

Confessing your faults one to another is important particularly for homeschool families. We spend so much time together that our faults become obvious anyway. If we don't confess them as faults, it opens the door for many problems. This is true between parents and children as well as between the children themselves. Prayer is a key ingredient to our school day, and we should pray often for each other. When we as homeschool moms make a mistake, it is good to ask the children to pray for us. It is hard to be humble in front of our children, but it is exactly what we must do as godly parents.

Our prayerful role model is very important. Mothers have much to pray about, and we should pray frequently. Our children learn from observing us praying. Ask the children not to interrupt you while you are praying. They will learn that this is a personal time between you and God. Pray out loud when they are in the room so they can hear your prayers some of the time. Let them know that you are praying for them that day. Pray specifically for the needs of that school day. Show them that it is God to whom we turn when we are in need of help.

Remember to offer your praise to God first, before your requests. Show your gratitude for your circumstances no matter how bad a day you are having. Fervent prayer works! Let your children know by your example just how much you rely on the truth of God's Word to guide you through the school day.

Have you prayed much today? Do your children know that you pray for them?

PRAYER

Dear Father, I feel awful. I know that I should pray and how powerful prayer is, but I forget. I try to do it in my own power and fail. I don't like to confess my faults to my husband, my children, or anyone. I'm not sure that my children realize that I do pray for them. When they see my head bowed and my eyes closed, they think I am sleeping. I need to take prayer more seriously. I am sorry that I have not been more faithful in my prayer life. I look to You for the grace to change. ❧

FOOD FOR THOUGHT

1. What distracts you from praying as often as you should? Establish some space in your home where you can minimize distractions and focus on your prayer life.
2. Teach your children to pray. Make sure they understand the importance of praise.
3. Begin a prayer journal and include it as a part of your daily devotions.

2 9

MOTHERS AREN'T SUPPOSED TO BE SICK

For our light affliction, which is but for a moment, worketh for us
a far more exceeding and eternal weight of glory.

2 CORINTHIANS 4:17

༄

*I*t was the twenty-ninth week of my pregnancy. I threw up all night and had diarrhea, too. The next day I was uncomfortable, weak, and nauseous. I had a headache. How do you take care of the family in such a condition? My husband had a day off and was home helping me. While trying to cheer me up, he tried to keep the boys quiet, clean up the three-year-old's accident on the way to the bathroom, and inform the one-and-a-half-year-old that he MUST stop screaming and take his nap.

This is not the only time that I have battled with incapacitating illness. It feels hopeless. It seems that there is no possible way to keep things going when Mom feels so bad. I have thought that mothers should not get sick while their children are young. On the contrary, I seem to pick up whatever virus they are exposed to. Ironically, it is at these times that my spiritual life takes a turn for the better.

When I am dealing with illness, I am once again reduced to helplessness. It is only then that Christ can truly be Lord of my life. Once I am completely dependent upon Him, He can do so much for me. It is during this time of helplessness that I more naturally turn to God. In turning to the Lord, I am responding well to my affliction, though it would be better if I turned frequently to God when I wasn't experiencing illness.

There are times when circumstances are brought about to teach us important truths. It is easy for our perspective to be poor when we are in the midst of a difficulty. It is possible to quickly sink into a pity party before we understand that our calamity is for our good. I don't like to be sick, but I have seen my self-reliant attitudes blown to pieces during these times, and I praise God for this. The illness itself can truly bring about spiritual growth if we keep God's perspective. Paul's words in 2 Corinthians 4:17 are most encouraging when we realize that our momentary struggle "worketh for us a far more exceeding and eternal weight of glory."

How do I handle the helpless feeling that comes when I am feeling very ill? To whom do I turn for help?

PRAYER

Father, I confess I am growing impatient with illness. I don't like to feel helpless and unable to keep my household running. I don't like being unable to control my circumstances. This must be exactly what I need in order to stop trying to run everything myself. Forgive me for missing the good teaching that these times of illness offer. I pray that our family may be healthy, but if we do become sick, please help me to see it from Your perspective. ◆

FOOD FOR THOUGHT

1. How have you responded to illness in your family when it upsets your daily routine?
2. Consider what God may be trying to teach you (that you haven't learned any other way) through an illness.
3. Develop a grateful heart for all circumstances by realizing that God uses them for our good.

3 0

WHY ARE YOU SO TIRED?

I can do all things through Christ which strengtheneth me.

PHILIPPIANS 4:13

❧

Strangers will often say, "How are you doing?" just to get the conversation going. Most people answer, "Fine." I say, "Tired." I try to eat well and get enough sleep. I exercise as often as possible. I am still tired. It may be because I am getting older. It could be because I have so many children. Whatever the cause, I saw something recently that helped me to understand why I am so tired.

We went to a tractor-pull, and I found it fascinating. Regular farm tractors were "enhanced," much like cars that are used for racing. These tractors were attached to a sled that dug into the ground, making it increasingly harder to pull. Each tractor tried to pull the sled the farthest. The last competition was between the biggest and most powerful tractors. The driver wore a fireproof suit and a helmet. When the tractors first began to pull, the front wheels of many of them lifted off the ground. I remember thinking that it was amazing that these farm tractors could perform the way they did. It was interesting that many of them developed mechanical problems and did not finish their pull.

I asked the man sitting next to me why so many of them broke down. His answer made a lot of sense. He said, "These tractors are doing three times the work they were designed to do." That is exactly how I feel. Just like the tractors, sometimes I do just fine pushing so hard, but other times I break down. It is exhausting to be surrounded by people who need me all day.

Babies awaken me at night. If I don't stop and recharge my batteries, eventually I won't be able to do my job too well.

I have learned that fatigue is a part of the program for me at this stage of life. Our days are full, and I am pushing myself each day. It is likely that I will feel tired. I am learning to rest. It may be only a few minutes, but this time is vital for me to keep going. If I glance at a magazine or sew for half an hour, I can be energized to tackle whatever comes next. Other times I may need to take a few naps or go to bed earlier. Planning times of rest is a positive response to the fatigue that will come. We should provide for this need without feeling guilty. It is in the quiet times of resting that we can draw on the Lord's strength.

Do you ever sit still? Do you seek your strength from the Lord?

PRAYER

Dear Jesus, how foolish I am to push so hard. No wonder I feel so tired. Help me to remember that it is through You that I gain the strength to complete my work. Give me wisdom to know just how much You would have me do each day. Help me to stop and rest daily. I know I can do the work if it is in Your strength that I do it. ❧

FOOD FOR THOUGHT

1. Are you feeling tired these days? What should you do about it?
2. Memorize Philippians 4:13 and say it aloud when you are exhausted.
3. Encourage your children to take a few minutes to rest each day.

3 1

A BIT OVERWHELMED?

Hide not thy face from me in the day when I am in trouble; incline thine ear unto me: in the day when I call answer me speedily.

PSALM 102:2

I don't know why major life changes occur in the fall when I am trying to get the school year started. Even though we have work to do all year long, the fall always seems like a new year starting. I probably am just having trouble letting go of memories of beginning school each September as a child. Nevertheless, my efforts to get us going are often influenced by significant distractions.

We have homeschooled for ten years. In that time I have had a baby in August, September, and two in October. I have moved in August and October. We started our home business in August. All of these events have brought great blessings to us. All of them have left me feeling overwhelmed.

I love to have a plan and know what is coming next. I thrive on the expected and try to stay calm when surprised. This fall was to be my "perfect" start to a new school year. I wasn't pregnant (the baby was four months old), I felt good, and I had exciting new curriculum and eager students. Best of all, I was feeling settled after we had decided to refinance our small home and remodel the kitchen. We decided this decorating project would be pretty stressful, so we were going to wait until the winter.

Exciting news came in mid-August as the opportunity to buy a ten-acre farm became a reality for us. Wow! I wasn't sure whether to be excited or to panic. The news was great, but what it required of me was far more than I could manage. Knowing full well that I needed to remain calm, I started to panic. Some days were smooth, but as moving day approached, it was wild. We had work to do on the new house and on our old house. I was in the middle of writing this devotional. One thought held me together: The Lord knew that we would be blessed with the farm when I was committed to writing this book. He knew I could handle it, so He must be the one I needed to ask how. I prayed often as I attempted to sort through the many details of each day. He did answer me speedily as things came together much easier in some ways than I had expected. I grew and I learned more when I was over-whelmed than I did when I had everything under control.

What is in your life that is pushing you beyond your limit? Turn to Jesus; He is the best help you can get.

PRAYER

Heavenly Father, thank You for being there for me. It scared me just to look at all I had to do and the short time in which it had to be done. I wouldn't have wanted to change it, but it was more than I could handle. How good You are to me to allow these times of stretching. I can see Your hand in so much more of my life at these times. Thank You for giving me so much on my plate. ❧

FOOD FOR THOUGHT

1. Identify what is overwhelming you.
2. Seek the Lord for help.
3. Enjoy the growth in your character.

3 2

I WANT . . .

*Let your conversation be without covetousness; and be content
with such things as ye have: for he hath said,
I will never leave thee, nor forsake thee.*

HEBREWS 13:5

❧

Why is it that we are never quite happy? Just when we become content with some area of our life, another area becomes a problem. Most of my homeschooling years I have lived in houses that were small for the number of people in our family and the way we were using the house. Finally the day came when I truly became content with my house. I stopped comparing the houses of other homeschooling families to my own. I stopped thinking about all of the very large homes in our community where all of the family either worked outside the home or went to school during the day. I stopped wanting their kitchens that were at least twice the size of my own. They probably didn't cook much anyway, so I thought. I gave up all of these thoughts, and in crept new thoughts.

I began to focus my attention on what others did not have. I wondered what people did with all of their time if they did not have children at home with them all day. It was not that I wanted to get rid of my children; I just wanted all of the time that I perceived childless couples as having. What dangerous thoughts these are to ever consider. The childless couple might very well be longing to be surrounded by children, as I am. Coveting the circumstances of someone else does not produce godly character. It breeds a never-ending dissatisfaction with life.

We should not view other parents in different circumstances as having it better than we do. We don't have all of the facts and aren't aware of all of their struggles. God designed our circumstances to fit our needs at just the right time. In wanting (coveting) what another person has, we are doubting God's wisdom in giving us what we have. I don't want to be in this position.

Whether we have a house that is too small or too big, or whether we have no children or what feels like too many, what really matters is whether we are where the Lord would have us be. God promises never to leave us or forsake us, and this promise is the most important consideration. What we have or don't have ceases to matter when we consider the glorious hope we have in the Lord Jesus Christ.

PRAYER

Thank You, Jesus, for being so near to me. What a comfort to know that You will never leave me. I think I need so many things in my life, but You are my sufficiency. Forgive me for wanting what other women have instead of gratefully acknowledging how much You have given to me. Thank You for the gift of so many children to train up in the way they should go. ❧

FOOD FOR THOUGHT

1. What sparks a covetous spirit in you? Houses? Decorating? Clothing? Take a hard look at these and praise God for what He has given to you.

2. Think about how you handle covetousness in your children. Help them to see that God provides just what He would want them to have each day.

3. Remember to thank God for your circumstances. He will never leave you or forsake you.

33

WHO IS GOING TO HELP DAD?

And the Lord God said, It is not good that the man should be alone; I will make him a help meet for him.

GENESIS 2:18

❧

I have no problem asking my husband to help me. I ask him often. I figure that he should help because there is so much to do. I suppose this is true, but that is not what this verse says. It tells me that I am to be *his* helper. Imagine that, after a busy day of schooling, laundry, meals, etc., I am to be available as his helper! When I first realized this, I became irritated.

It doesn't seem fair. After all, I am just so busy with the family. How can I find time to help my husband? Wow! What misplaced priorities I had. While I found it easy to ask him to help me, I had completely failed to help him in his areas of responsibility. Finally I changed this situation.

It seems to take forever to get any decorating done in our home. I don't know much about painting and wallpaper, so I thought my husband could just do it himself. I was slow to realize that I could and *should* learn how to help him. One winter we took wallpaper off the walls in a bathroom and a bedroom. Within a week we had both rooms painted and finished. I was surprised at how quickly we had completed the project together.

The fact that I was helping him made all the difference. It was a break for me, too. We spent time together working and set our usual duties aside temporarily. I was filling my proper role as a wife, and it worked. So often I get busy and forget to offer to help my husband. God says that this is my job. The reason he made me (a woman) was because my husband (a man) needed help. The very least I can do is follow this plan without resisting.

Do you help your husband often? What more could you do to be his helper?

PRAYER

Father, I confess to You that I am a slow learner. I have been aware of my role as a helpmeet to my husband but haven't really understood what that meant. I have selfishly asked for his help and offered none in return. What a poor role model I have been for my daughters. Help me to look for opportunities to help him. Energize me for these tasks. ❧

FOOD FOR THOUGHT

1. Make a list of the areas where you believe that your husband could use your help. Have him look over your list and make any necessary corrections. Plan some times where the two of you work together on something for him.

2. Give your husband a chance to look over your "to-do" list. Have him add anything that he would like you to help him do.

3. Reflect upon what our culture says about a woman's role. Praise God for giving you such a special role as a wife. Rejoice each time you are truly a helpmeet to your husband. You are following God's plan for women.

34

I'M A BAD MOTHER

*And these words, which I command thee this day, shall be in
thine heart: And thou shalt teach them diligently unto thy children,
and shalt talk of them when thou sittest in thine house,
and when thou walkest by the way, and when thou
liest down, and when thou risest up.*

DEUTERONOMY 6:6-7

I don't like to read bedtime stories. That sounds terrible, but it is how I
feel. I spend all day interacting with my children. Stories are read during the
day. When day is done and it is time for bed, I don't have anything left to
read a story. I do read at bedtime once in a while, but it is the exception to
the rule. I had no problem with this until my children became aware of
other children hearing a bedtime story.

I felt like a bad mother. My children wanted to know why we did not
have bedtime stories, and they asked for them for some time. I just don't
have the energy at bedtime. I felt guilty about this for quite a while. Bedtime
stories seem to be part of good parenting from as far back as I can remember. Reading is an excellent way to end the day with your child. This routine
in many homes makes going to bed fun for the children. I still can't bring
myself to do this. Does this make me a bad mother?

Fortunately Deuteronomy 6:6-7 explains my situation. In other homes,
parents and children go their separate ways during the day, and in some
instances bedtime is the first time all day they have had a chance to talk to

each other. It makes sense to guard this time and make it special. But home-schooling moms are with their children for most of their waking hours. We don't necessarily need a time in the evening to check in with each other. We have been together and experiencing the day side by side. We have already had plenty of time to read stories.

The teaching and training of our children happens all of the time. It doesn't get slotted into school hours or specific times of study. Homeschooling is a lifestyle of training our children in godliness, which includes character training, academics, and life skills. How and when you will teach these is up to you. Don't let the habits of other families restrict your own routines. Do what makes sense for your family and do it to the glory of God.

Are you feeling guilty? Should you be?

PRAYER

Father, thank You for allowing me so much time each day with my children. Help me to make better use of this time and read to them often. I sometimes feel guilty when I do things differently from others. Help me to see Your will for our family and not look at what other families are doing. Keep me focused on the methods that work best for our situation. ❧

FOOD FOR THOUGHT

1. What are you failing to do for your children that makes you feel guilty.
2. Is someone else making you feel this way, or are you doing it to yourself?
3. Seek God's will in this area and discern what His best is for you. Lay aside input from others that makes you feel guilty.

3 5

I DON'T KNOW HOW TO DO THIS!

And he said unto me, My grace is sufficient for thee:
for my strength is made perfect in weakness. Most gladly
therefore will I rather glory in my infirmities, that
the power of Christ may rest upon me.

2 CORINTHIANS 12:9

❧

I was talking to a woman in the parking lot at the grocery store. She was
curious about how many seats were in my van. She has a large family, too.
We started talking about other things, and she asked me if we homeschooled.
When I responded that we did, she said, "Oh, everybody homeschools. I
could never do that." I found her comment interesting. She obviously knew
other homeschoolers, and I could tell by the tone of her voice that she wished
she could do it, too. She commented that I must have a lot of patience. I
told her it was something I was learning on the job.

It is humorous to me that so many women think I have some special
gifting that makes me able to homeschool. No way! There are so many times
that I feel completely inadequate for the task and wonder what to do next. I
am uncertain of my ability to juggle high school level work, elementary
grades, a new reader, an eager preschooler, an active toddler, and a darling
baby. Many days I question whether I have what it takes.

That is just where God wants me to be. How can God work in my life
when I feel I can handle everything by myself? If I felt completely capable of
managing our homeschool, I would not need God for anything. When I first

started homeschooling, I felt pretty confident. Teaching kindergarten to one child was manageable. Now my situation is bigger than I am. How much better this is for me because I must look to the Lord.

I enjoy 2 Corinthians 12:9 because this verse gives me permission to feel inadequate. We are told to glory in our infirmities because it is at this time we will have the power of Christ resting upon us. More will be accomplished in your school when the Lord is directing than at any other time. I don't like feeling inadequate, but I don't believe I am cut out for homeschooling any more than the woman I spoke with at the grocery store. It is only by the grace of God that I am able to do what I do.

Are you sure you can handle homeschooling? Me neither.

PRAYER

God, You are so good to me. You have given me a task that is far greater than my own abilities. You have allowed me to thrive in spite of my inadequacies. You have touched our family in a special way by showing me that it is You who has the power to make this work. It is not me. I am just the instrument You are using to educate my children. Thank You for doing a great job! ❧

FOOD FOR THOUGHT

1. Make a list of all of the inadequacies that you feel are hampering your homeschooling efforts. Seek the Lord's direction in these areas.

2. Reflect on your attitude toward your weak areas. How does God's promise to make His strength perfect in your weakness change the way you should view your weaknesses?

3. Praise God for a perfect Jesus.

NO MORE TRIALS, PLEASE

And we know that all things work together for good to them that love God, to them who are the called according to his purpose.

ROMANS 8:28

❧

I think it is our nature to want to avoid trials and struggles. They are demanding and require much of us. It is much easier when everything is running smoothly. At least, if trials are going to come, let them come one at a time so we can handle them well. Our family had one entire year that would just not ease up. Struggles were mounting two and three deep, and my response to them began to deteriorate. It was here that I began to see some great life-skill teaching take place in our home.

My most difficult pregnancy was preceded by a miscarriage and followed by a move 100 miles away. Various other issues cropped up to make this a trying time. When I am under pressure, and especially when I am not feeling well, I don't always respond appropriately to my children. I tend to overreact and criticize. My oldest child, Jamie, is usually the recipient of my wrong reactions.

One time when I was too critical of her during this stressful year, her response was beautiful. When I apologized to Jamie, I could see that she had not taken my comments personally. I explained to her that during times of stress I do not always respond properly. She had already figured this out and did not let my comments hurt her. What a teachable moment! I saw a maturity beyond her years and realized something good had come of a bad situation.

I do not advocate behaving badly on purpose to create a teaching tool. But I do see God using the trials in our home as powerful examples to our children. Jamie is learning a valuable life skill when she is able to respond properly to people who are not treating her well. How many times in adult life will she be confronted with a similar situation? I wish I had learned this skill when I was a child. It has been harder to learn as an adult.

Trials don't interrupt the schedule; they *are* the schedule. Remember that even in the worst of times, there is some good in it for your family, and that is God's promise to those who love Him.

Are trials overwhelming you now? Seek the good in them and allow God to bless you through the trial.

PRAYER

Dear God, thank You for the lessons I learn from my children. I was humbled by Jamie's godly response to my failure. She is an example to me, and I believe that You do use all things to work for our good. Help me to remember this when I am in the middle of challenging circumstances. Let our trials be some of the best teaching times and keep me from running from them. Show me how to get the most out of all that You bring into my life. ❧

FOOD FOR THOUGHT

1. Do you welcome the trials, knowing that they will work together for good because you are called according to God's purpose?
2. Have you taken the time to use trials and struggles as teaching tools?
3. Have your entire family memorize Romans 8:28.

3 7

WHERE ARE WE GOING?

And be not conformed to this world: but be ye transformed by the
renewing of your mind, that ye may prove what is that good,
and acceptable, and perfect will of God.

ROMANS 12:2

~

God created all of us with a specific purpose in mind. I believe that each homeschool has a divine purpose, too. The children that you are educating will be influenced by your strengths and weaknesses. This is no accident. Some families may turn out a fair number of doctors while another has construction workers. Other families may have girls with strong homemaking skills or daughters who are career-minded. Whatever your (and your husband's) strengths are, you can be sure that the Lord intends to use them in the training of your children.

When I first began to homeschool, I craved fellowship with other homeschoolers. One family we visited often was highly academic. The children were dissecting animal brains in first grade. This family made me nervous. I left our visits feeling that my efforts could not measure up to the work they were doing in their school. Our objectives are more character-oriented. Academics are important, but they are not the focal point. Our elementary-aged children learn the basics of reading, writing, and arithmetic in preparation for higher learning. Character training is our focus, particularly in the early years.

There is nothing wrong with our approach or that of my friend. The problem came when I kept comparing what I was doing to what she was doing. Our homeschools should not look alike. God's plan for each family will dictate what the school looks like. We should be certain and settled about what we are doing, using the Bible as our guide. Our lifestyle should reflect God's will for our own particular family.

It is difficult to forget about what others are doing, and yet it is important that we do not conform to what we see around us. We must seek renewal from God so that we can see what His will is for *us*. It helps me to know why we are homeschooling and what our goals are when we are finished. It is okay if my school looks different from yours. God doesn't want us all to be the same. Seek His will and make that the cornerstone of your curriculum.

Do you feel uncomfortable when other homeschoolers are using a completely different approach from yours?

PRAYER

Jesus, thank You for diversity. Thank You for giving us different plans for the education of our children. Some will need strong people skills while others will need sharp math skills. We don't all grow up to serve the same function, and it makes sense that the training process for each person is not the same. Help me not to feel threatened by those who are stronger in some area than I am. Show me my strengths and let me use them to further Your kingdom through the educating of my children. ⨾

FOOD FOR THOUGHT

1. Do you know God's will for *your* homeschool? Pray about this with your family.

2. Enjoy the diversity among homeschooling families without needing to be just like other families. Thank God for the specific plan He has for your family.

3. Identify the strengths in each family member. Is there a pattern? Design your curriculum around the direction that the Lord is leading each one of your children.

38

CHILD TRAINING 101

Chasten thy son while there is hope, and
let not thy soul spare for his crying.

PROVERBS 19:18

❧

We took a camping vacation recently to one of my favorite places. We stayed in a campground located in an Amish area in Indiana. I love to go there because life slows down, and I find it a peaceful place to be. The campground has enough for the children to do, and usually everyone is happy.

When we are on vacation, the children are usually on their best behavior. That was not the case this trip. Their disobedience ruined the vacation for me. Part of the problem was that one of our children was two years old. This time in the life of children is critical to their future development. We are wise parents to take the time at this age to train them properly, which lays the foundation for future success in the teen years. Knowing this, I still had failed to be consistent enough with this child, and his behavior on the trip was wild. He had gotten away with too much for too long. We must be consistent in requiring prompt, cheerful obedience from children regardless of what they think. At times this becomes a full-time job.

Even the older children were a bit difficult. Following directions seemed impossible for them, and there was a lot of parental follow-up. I finally decided after a few days that if all we were going to do was deal with constant child-training issues, we should have stayed home. Their misbehavior was our fault to some degree because we had failed to require them to obey consistently.

I give in too often to their crying and fail to follow through with discipline. Their behavior suffers for it. Chastening needs to occur swiftly after the child has disobeyed. It takes much effort on the parent's part to be consistent, but the rewards for both child and parent are worth it.

Are your children obedient? Have you required them to be obedient?

PRAYER

Lord, I feel like a failure in the parenting department. I know what I should do, but I have such a tough time following through and doing it correctly. Help me to be more consistent and require my children to obey at an early age. How helpful this training will be as they grow up and learn to obey Your commands. Give me the strength to keep up with the needs of my children. It is my heart's desire to do this right. ✒

FOOD FOR THOUGHT

1. Get a copy of *Proverbs for Parenting* and study what the Bible says about child-training.
2. Consider teaching obedience from the very beginning of your children's toddler years. Various curricula exist, and there are Bible studies on obedience for the older children. This is crucial to all areas of life and should top the list of required courses in your school.
3. Reflect on your own track record of obedience. Did you obey your parents? Do you follow your husband? Does God direct your steps? Commit yourself to address any areas where you are failing. The role model of obedience that you set for your children is observed by them all day long. It is important that we model the right behaviors and attitudes.

39

A Child of Virtue

*And besides this, giving all diligence, add to your
faith virtue; and to virtue, knowledge.*

2 PETER 1:5

≈✝

The moral climate in our culture has made a statement about character. Apparently increasing numbers of people believe that a person's character doesn't matter. This is simply not true. Peter is talking about life and godliness in this verse, and it is interesting to note that virtue comes before knowledge in the order of importance. This means that while character training (virtue) and knowledge (academics) are both important, character training is of the utmost importance.

Children need to know what godly character is and see examples of it. We read books about people who exhibit the character traits we want to see in our children. Our readers are filled with stories that teach godly character. Examples of godly character can be found in the people around us, and these, too, serve as examples for our children. It helps if they see godly character in Mom and Dad, too.

I have a curriculum that specifically teaches character, but more often than not, we learn through the experiences of the day. When one child aggravates another, we teach why that behavior is wrong. If a child takes another child's belongings, we call it stealing and teach why it is wrong. When a child lies, we take it seriously and teach the child not to do it again. Teaching in this way sounds simple, but it becomes challenging when these teachable moments occur over and over. It would seem at times that I teach the same thing constantly. Godly character is not produced overnight, and we must be diligent in teaching it.

Godly character is not achieved through satisfying the desires of the flesh. Christ's flawless example of how we should live is our model. While tempted in the same ways that we are, He was without sin. Reading through the Gospels (Matthew, Mark, Luke, and John) with your children can provide some powerful examples of the character qualities that you desire for them and for yourself.

While we purposefully train for character in our home, I find that my own character needs some help. It is most effective if the teacher models the desired behavior for the students. Praise God that we have Jesus to help us in this pursuit of excellence!

Do your children show signs of godly character? Praise them often for all of the good character qualities that you see.

PRAYER

Lord, I confess to You that while I have taught character to my children for years, I have recently observed that I am a character. There are some areas of my life that really need Your help. My example to my children isn't always the best. Help me to be the mom You want me to be. I want to let go of my fleshly responses and model good character qualities for them. Please work quickly in me, Lord, because they are growing up fast. ✧

FOOD FOR THOUGHT

1. Keep informed of your child's character development by asking him or her questions frequently. Jesus asked the disciples questions often, and He knew from their answers what they understood.
2. Treat yourself to a book about a woman of noble character.
3. Remember that sanctification (becoming more like Jesus) is something that takes a lifetime. Godly character development in children takes time.

40

KNOWLEDGE IS GOOD

*The heart of the prudent getteth knowledge; and
the ear of the wise seeketh knowledge.*

PROVERBS 18:15

❦

Worldwide access to vast amounts of information on the Internet has raised new questions in my mind about how much knowledge we need. There is so much available to us that it is easy to have more than we could ever use. Information is not bad, but accumulating it just so you have it sounds like a new clutter problem. It makes the task of deciding what you really need to know much harder.

It is not possible to study everything anymore. There is too much information available for children to process. What do they really need to know? The answer to this question affects what I teach them. I remember when I took typing in high school. We spent a lot of time practicing to increase our speed. When it came time to get a job, typing speed had an effect on how much a person was paid. Now as I type on my computer, my speed is much faster than it ever was on the typewriter. Once I learned the keyboard, the extra time I spent practicing my typing speed didn't matter eventually.

So how do I decide what to teach? I keep coming back to the same conclusion—teach the children how to learn. I can't know for sure what they will need in the future. Technology changes so quickly that what they learn today may be obsolete tomorrow. I teach them the fundamentals in the first few years of schooling. Other subjects are taught with a focus on learning how to learn on their own. They will need to learn for the rest of their lives, and I believe they will need to upgrade their skills and knowledge more frequently than we adults do.

It is good for our children to learn knowledge. It is wise to encourage them to learn all they can in their special areas of interest. At the same time we must teach them to limit how much knowledge they seek. Have you ever had so many options that it was impossible to make a good decision without limiting those options? Just try to select a box of cereal at the grocery store, and you will see what I mean. Knowledge is not bad. The Bible says it is good. How we use the knowledge we have is the true test of its usefulness. Application of information is more important than just getting the information.

Is your household on information overload? Narrow your scope for a day or two and see what happens.

PRAYER

Father, I cannot possibly figure out what information You would desire my children to know. There are so many good subjects to study and finite amounts of time. Help me to see Your plan for each of my children so that I spend enough time on the right topics to prepare them for life. Keep me aware of the skills that they will need in our changing world. Thank You for the opportunity to equip my children for their future. ❧

FOOD FOR THOUGHT

1. Evaluate your children in terms of their potential. Discuss as a family what types of skills will be necessary for their future.
2. Tailor your curriculum to meet these needs.
3. Pray for guidance to know what knowledge will be critical for them to know.

4 1

I WANT TO TALK TO AN ADULT

But if we walk in the light, as he is in the light, we have
fellowship one with another, and the blood of
Jesus Christ his Son cleanseth us from all sin.

1 JOHN 1:7

I am amazed at how often I hear about the "problem" of socialization and homeschoolers. Apparently there are still many who believe that homeschoolers are sequestered in their homes away from other human beings and therefore never develop the interpersonal skills so vital to a well-rounded life. This isn't true. Most homeschoolers are at ease with a variety of ages and exhibit very effective interpersonal skills. Many of them are excellent communicators. I don't worry about the socialization of homeschoolers, but I am concerned about the social life of their mothers.

I enjoy talking to my children. I learn a lot about them and from them. They are some of the most interesting people I have met. But there comes a time each day when I really don't want to speak with them anymore. I want to talk to an adult. I want to talk about what is going on in the world. I want to be with one of my peers. It is the homeschooling mothers who end up isolated and lonely if they are not careful. They are the ones who have trouble with social skills if they don't make a point of being with other adults. How embarrassed I would be if in adult company I asked if anyone had to go potty. It *could* happen.

I like to fellowship with other women. I can learn so much in just a few minutes of dialogue. It is good for us to get together with other homeschool moms. I have one friend that used to attend the same church we did. When we get to talking about curriculum (we both teach using the same style), I invariably learn of a new book or two I should read. I have gotten some of my best material in short conversations with my friend. She in turn has observed our family and implemented some of what we do in her own home successfully. The exchange of ideas never stops. Although I don't see my friend very often anymore, our visits are precious and treasured.

I have found it painful when friends have moved away. It seems that just when I get close to someone, she moves away. I once considered giving up on friendships because this is so hard on me. There is a better way. I need to shift my human craving for people to a craving to spend more time with my Lord who can meet my deepest needs. If we rely on the fellowship with friends to meet all of our needs, then we shut out the Lord. Some of my very best friends are the ones who point me to Christ.

Have you seen your friends lately? It's okay—go out for a snack together.

PRAYER

Father, I thank You for my friends. I am grateful for the encouragement that I receive from fellow homeschool moms who understand the challenges I face. ✧

FOOD FOR THOUGHT

1. Pray for your friends regularly.
2. Discuss why fellowship with other Christians is important.
3. Consider setting aside time each week for fellowship. Invite a family over. Have tea with the mother by yourself on another day.

4 2

BABIES, BABIES, BABIES

And he said, About this season, according to the time of life,
thou shalt embrace a son. And she said, Nay, my lord, thou man
of God, do not lie unto thine handmaid. And the woman
conceived, and bare a son at that season that Elisha
had said unto her, according to the time of life.

2 KINGS 4:16-17

I enjoy my babies. They are about the cutest things I have ever seen. Even though raising children is quite a challenge, I welcome the opportunity to raise as many as God will give us. I get quite a few hostile comments on our family size. I once met with a godly woman in her seventies who had five children. A friend of mine would accompany me to her home where we studied the biblical foundations of marriage. I found it helpful because this woman always turned to Scripture for the answers to my questions. Then one day she told me that the Bible did not have everything spelled out clearly. She told me there were gray areas. It was, of course, over the issue of children.

At the time I had five children. I mentioned the possibility of another child, and this woman grew hostile. She told me that I had better "use my head" and made some other choice comments. I showed her the verses that indicate children are a blessing, but these did not move her. Difficult as this was, I was astonished when my friend, who was the oldest of seven, joined in to condemn what I know is scriptural. Both friendships have dissolved, and I learned how touchy this subject can be with some people.

Pregnancy can be a long and difficult process. It doesn't help when fellow Christians feel free to criticize God's decision to allow you to carry a child. My seventh pregnancy was the hardest. I was happy about it and looked forward to a new baby. As the fatigue and discomfort continued throughout the entire nine months, my enthusiasm waned. I developed an attitude toward pregnancy that did not reflect any appreciation for the gift that God was giving me. The labor and delivery were my most difficult, and the recovery was the same story.

But it was just as special as ever to have a new baby. At a few months old, Julianne and I had a little routine early in the morning. I would bring her in bed with me, and for a few minutes she would gaze into my eyes with a big smile. To her I was everything. She would then doze off next to me, and sometimes I would stay awake and watch her. God makes no mistakes. She is a gift and was well worth what I went through for her to be a part of our family.

Children *are* a gift. The Shunammite woman received a son in her husband's old age as a reward for her service to Elisha.

Do you welcome children as a blessing? Should you?

PRAYER

Father, thank You for blessing me with so many children. I don't feel worthy of so many gifts. Thank You. ❧

FOOD FOR THOUGHT

1. Read Psalm 127.
2. Tell your children they are a gift from God to you. Make each one feel special.
3. Find a large homeschooling family and praise them for allowing God to bless them.

4 3

ENOUGH TO GO AROUND

And he took the seven loaves and the fishes, and gave thanks,
and brake them, and gave to his disciples, and the disciples to the
multitude. And they did all eat, and were filled: and they took up
of the broken meat that was left seven baskets full. And they that
did eat were four thousand men, beside women and children.

MATTHEW 15:36-38

Meeting multilevel needs in your homeschool is no easy task. It becomes more challenging as more levels are demanding your attention at once. I have found it impossible at times to make this work well. I have decided that due to using the wrong methods, I have missed the blessings of unique solutions to these challenges.

Jesus had a large group of people that needed to be fed. Only a few fish and seven loaves were available. It hardly seemed enough for the thousands of hungry people needing a meal. Jesus solved the problem in a unique way. He did not use a conventional method. He did not go to the neighboring markets and buy up all of their food. His way was easier and faster. We don't know exactly how Jesus did it, but it worked, and it worked well.

Unique approaches work in the homeschool. One day I was not able to work with my young boys as I had planned. Instead I asked Jimmy (age seven) to work with Jonathan (age five) on his math. This reinforced the concepts for Jimmy and strengthened the bond between the brothers. As I watched this from a distance, I wondered what was more important that day, math concepts or the closeness being fostered in their relationship. I was encouraged by their progress.

Jesus can work a miracle in your homeschool. As you seek Him in your approach to meeting the needs of all of your children, you may be surprised. "For my thoughts are not your thoughts, neither are your ways my ways, saith the LORD" (Isa. 55:8). There are special opportunities open to you if you will allow the Lord to allocate your time. Some days I don't know *how* I accomplished so much in our schoolwork for that day. I know that those are the days I relied on the Lord. When my own plans for juggling it all are in place, I don't see such progress.

Are you unsure of how you (the limited resource) will take care of the needs of the multitude (your children)? Seek Jesus—He had overwhelming needs to meet too.

PRAYER

Heavenly Father, I confess to You that I don't see a way that I can possibly meet all of the various needs of the many ages represented by our children. This concerns me, and I need Your help. Remind me of the loaves and the fishes so I remember that You do work miracles. I believe that You can lead me in a way that uniquely meets the needs in our family. I need You. ❧

FOOD FOR THOUGHT

1. Identify your greatest stumbling blocks to meeting the multilevel needs in your home effectively.
2. Ask for help where help is needed.
3. Observe the methods other families are using to get the job done. Ask questions about how they do it. Keep an open mind as to how you can implement some of these ideas in your own home. Modify them to suit your specific situation.

44

I AM HAPPY

*Not that I speak in respect of want: for I have learned, in
whatsoever state I am, therewith to be content.*

PHILIPPIANS 4:11

❧

Wouldn't it be nice if children learned everything they were taught every
day? It would be nice also if parents learned everything God wanted to teach
them every day. It won't happen. Most of us have not been able to apply
what we know already. We all have much to learn.

Why, then, am I so frustrated when one of my children struggles with
learning a new concept or exhibiting desirable character qualities on a consistent basis? One of my girls has trouble finishing a task completely. Although
she has taken on much responsibility, I tend to look more at the unfinished
work and wonder why she isn't done. I have totally missed the point here. My
work is to instruct this child in task completion and follow through until
she does it correctly on her own. It should be a joy for me to teach her these
things and a privilege to watch her progress. Instead I fuss over the fact that
she still can't get it right.

It is so easy for us to miss the important and focus on the nonessentials.
This happens when we are not content. We keep wanting something to be different. We wish that our children would just learn faster, like our friend's children. Unfortunately we have missed the blessing of diligently working with
the child who needs extra help or attention.

In choosing to be content, we respect God's judgment regarding our
circumstances. We affirm that we believe He knows what we need at any given

moment. I need the character growth that comes from being required to follow up so closely with my daughter. Follow-up is one of my weaker areas. Isn't it perfect that our Lord would allow me a situation that would force me to learn to follow up more effectively? I am slow to learn, but I am beginning to see that my daughter needs to be trained more than she needs me to criticize her poor performance.

Isn't that just the way Jesus works in our lives? The Bible shows us how to live, and yet we are slow to understand how to implement the teaching found in this great book. Our Lord is patient and loving as He must teach us the same things over and over again. Eventually we catch on and we learn.

Do you have a child who is struggling in some area? Have you seen this struggle as an opportunity and made the decision to be content with the circumstances?

PRAYER

Dear Lord, forgive my impatient nature. I want everything to run smoothly. I expect the jobs to be done well. I forget that I am in the middle of training my children to do these things. They are in process and are not through learning. Neither am I. Thank You for being so patient with me when I don't learn very well. Let me be just the same way with my children. ❧

FOOD FOR THOUGHT

1. Can you accept great challenges in your homeschooling efforts and be content with the situation? Why or why not?
2. Memorize Philippians 4:11.
3. List all of the areas in your life where you are not content. Be honest. Pray for direction in how to change your attitude.

IT WAS FREE

Every man according as he purposeth in his heart, so let him give;
not grudgingly, or of necessity: for God loveth a cheerful giver.

2 CORINTHIANS 9:7

I am an avid garage-sale shopper. There are certain items I seek when I go garage-saling. Beyond terrific savings on boy's jeans, I come home with furniture, tools, craft supplies, and more. I estimate that I have saved hundreds of dollars, if not thousands. The fine china with place settings for twelve was worth over $1,000. I paid $75. Recently I was given a beautiful denim dress at a garage sale—free!

I get satisfaction from meeting the needs of the family without spending a lot of money. I feel frugal each time I pay much less for something than it cost new. Sometimes the item is new with tags still on. Being frugal is different from being cheap. Being too cheap means you aren't willing to spend your money on anything. Being frugal means that you are wise in the spending of your money. You seek the most for the least amount of money.

I have had people question whether the time spent at garage sales really pays off. They reason that you spend more time looking for what you need. I say that it pays off. I spend less time and get much more—for a fraction of what items would cost in a department store. This dollar savings is important to us in two ways. I feel that I am a better steward of the money that we have when I shop garage sales. While I don't find everything we need this way, I do get most of our needs (and wants) satisfied. The second reason is the most important.

When I spend less money to meet our own needs, I am creating extra money that is available to help others. If our budget was very tight, we would not have anything to give. This way we have resources to meet the needs of others. It is economical to find something for a friend at a garage sale, and this allows us another way to be generous.

Have you given to anyone lately? Do you have the resources?

PRAYER

Father, thank You for showing me ways to be frugal. I am amazed at how much "extra" money we have when I shop wisely. Help us to know who needs our help. You have provided abundantly for us, and we desire to share with those in need. ❧

FOOD FOR THOUGHT

1. Do you take the extra time to shop wisely for the needs of your family? Keep track of your expenditures for one month, including how much you save shopping sales, garage sales, etc. Estimate how much extra money you have as a result of being frugal. Select a missionary to whom you would like to give this money.

2. Discuss giving with your children. Look up words such as *grudgingly* and *necessity* from 2 Corinthians 9:7. Study the meaning of this passage.

3. Consider ways your family can be more giving. Do you have toys that you no longer need? Could you help another family with a project in their home? Find ways to serve the needy in your community during the holidays. Praise God for the opportunity to teach your children how to give while they are young!

4 6

I WANT IT NOW!

Be patient therefore, brethren, unto the coming of the Lord.
Behold, the husbandman waiteth for the precious fruit of the earth,
and hath long patience for it, until he receive the early and
latter rain. Be ye also patient; stablish your hearts:
for the coming of the Lord draweth nigh.

JAMES 5:7-8

I am puzzled by the number of people who have told me that I must have a lot of patience to homeschool. Oh, how I wish this were true. I have more patience now than I did when I started, but this is not nearly enough. The process of homeschooling develops over time, which makes my unreasonable desire for immediate results impossible. I want my children to get their work done correctly the first time, follow directions to the letter, and do their work without being told. I want strong readers with good math skills. I want to be calm, cool, and collected all of the time.

It is true that I am aiming high. That is okay as long as I remember that it will take time to achieve these goals. Some may never be achieved, but at least progress is a desirable objective. The only problem is that I must wait. Waiting for results is the most frustrating experience when you want them *now*. Homeschool is such a good environment in which to learn to be patient. I am not able to homeschool because I am patient. Homeschooling is what is developing the patience in me.

I understand the patience of a farmer now that I live in the country.

Having been a city girl all of my life, this has been a great opportunity to understand waiting. I have always enjoyed the harvest season. Although harvest is fairly short, the preparation for it goes on for many months. Once the spring planting is finished, time must pass for the plants to grow. Sun, rain, good soil, and many other factors influence the harvest.

So it goes with homeschooling. First it takes time for your child to learn to read. Then his reading skills need to be practiced. Good literature and non-fiction books will enhance his mind. Character training and life-skill development are important components. Biblical principles applied to all of life greatly increase the harvest. But it takes time. Sometimes it takes a long time. The process of waiting is good for you. It will develop patience in you if you allow it to bless you rather than frustrate you.

Are you impatient with your children? With yourself?

PRAYER

Father, I don't feel very patient. I have my timetables and my agendas and my expectations. I don't like to wait. I want it now. Help me to see the futility in this kind of thinking. Show me how to think the way You do. Help me to see the wisdom in developing greater patience. ✑

FOOD FOR THOUGHT

1. In what aspect of your homeschooling are you the most impatient? Why?
2. Observe your children and determine what makes them impatient. Ask them questions about how they feel when they have to wait. Evaluate their answers in terms of how you feel. Is there an obvious area that you can begin to work on ?
3. Consider the blessings of having to wait. The only way to develop more patience is to have to wait for something. Isn't it worth it?

WHERE DID THE TIME GO?

And on the seventh day God ended his work which he had made;
and he rested on the seventh day from all his work which he had made.
And God blessed the seventh day, and sanctified it: because that in
it he had rested from all his work which God created and made.

GENESIS 2:2-3

I wonder why time is so precious in midlife. I remember clock-watching in my earlier years. I was waiting for class to end or 5:00 P.M. to come so my working day would be over. There was such an abundance of time back then. Now it seems I never have enough time to do what I want to do. I really would like to do some sewing, but quality clothing costs less at garage sales than the fabric to make them. It doesn't make sense to spend time sewing, or does it?

I get satisfaction out of being creative when I sew. I can sew for hours without even realizing it is time for a meal. Sometimes I just need to set aside time to work on a project at the sewing machine. I can devote every waking moment to my homeschooling endeavors if I choose to do so. There will always be more for me to do. It is better for me to spend a little time sewing. It recharges my batteries. I believe that this is God's best for me some of the time.

God created the world in six days. He rested on the seventh day. If God made time for rest, then we must, too. God blessed His day of rest in which He did not complete any more work. While I do make provisions for Sundays to be as much a day of rest as possible, there are other times during the week when I really need to rest from my work. There is enough time. If God had enough time to get His work done, then so do we.

Time is precious. We must use it wisely, or we will end our days with little to show for the time we were allowed to educate our children at home. There are some things that we must do and others that we would like to do. Just because we are homeschooling doesn't mean that we must give up all that we want to do. Balancing these choices is a challenge, but it will benefit your family as you realize that you do have enough time.

What do you like to do that you have not done in a long time? Do it!

PRAYER

Father, I confess that I complain too much that I don't have enough time. I have as much time as You have given me. Not only should this be sufficient but more than enough if I choose wisely how to spend this time. Help me to see the most important work and spend my time on what matters. Show me those moments when I can rest and refocus. Thank You for giving me so much time. ❧

FOOD FOR THOUGHT

1. If you had more time, what would you do with it? Can you rearrange your schedule so that you have enough time? How?
2. Determine whether disorganization is stealing your time. Set up some new systems in your home to streamline what you are doing.
3. Praise God for time to rest.

4 8

STRESS KILLS

*Take therefore no thought for the morrow: for the morrow
shall take thought for the things of itself. Sufficient
unto the day is the evil thereof.*

MATTHEW 6:34

❦

A popular phrase when I was growing up was "Speed kills"—a reminder to people to slow their cars down on the highway. Stress kills too. The dangers of stress in relation to your health are well documented. Many times a day stress can be wearing us down physically, emotionally, and spiritually without our knowing it. I know. It nearly did me in one day.

Less than a week after we moved to our farmhouse, I was not managing stress well. We doubled the size of our living space with this move, and I was in the middle of unpacking essentials such as clothing. The long staircase leading to the upstairs became my enemy as I was running up and down with laundry, boxes, and children calling for me from the first floor. For every item I unpacked there seemed to be another situation that needed my attention. Frustrated with my slow progress, my mind wandered to the plumbing problem we were experiencing in the kitchen. Our schoolroom was still filled with boxes, and as we ended the month of October, we still hadn't officially begun our fall routine. The many details that I had not yet worked out were overwhelming me.

Oh, how I needed perspective that day. I was borrowing trouble for other days. In reality, I did accomplish enough for that day. My desire was to do more, but the needs of the children limited my efforts. That was just fine. The move was stressful for me, and I had set up unrealistic expectations for getting settled in. The attitude that I needed to have was one of taking as much time as I needed to get settled. No deadlines, no comparisons to other moves, no thoughts of other people I know who move often and seem to have few problems.

It is easy to get bogged down by the great number of things that we as homeschoolers juggle all of the time. We can manage to keep it all going some of the time, but for all of us, there comes a time where it all crashes. We can't keep the schedule working, or we aren't getting healthy food on the table regularly. Our laundry threatens to consume us. For me, moving from the suburbs to the country was a big change that sent all of my systems off track for a time while I got my bearings in my new home. When Jesus said that we should take no thought of tomorrow, He said it for us. He meant it for today! The needs of this day are enough to handle.

How are you handling stress today? Give your concerns to Jesus.

PRAYER

Heavenly Father, thank You for being patient with me. I fuss and fret over many things. You know my needs even before I do. I know You can meet them. Forgive me for being concerned about the things that You can take care of for me. Help me to relax in the comfort of Your care. ❧

FOOD FOR THOUGHT

1. List *all* of the stressors in your life.
2. List ten things you like to do to relax.
3. Do one today!

4 9

PASSING THE WISDOM TEST

*for wisdom is better than rubies; and all the things that
may be desired are not to be compared to it.*

PROVERBS 8:11

∞

When I first began homeschooling, I was very concerned that I would
not "cover" everything. I was thinking in terms of what I remember of my own
education. I thought that homeschooling would entail facilitating the right
environment so my children would learn everything they possibly could.
While this is true, learning information without knowing what to do with it
is incomplete education.

I did well in school. I graduated very near the top of my class. My grades
were mostly A's and B's. I was able to pass tests with flying colors. A perfect
paper was not uncommon for me. My grades were looked at as an indicator
of how smart I was at the time. My test scores proved it. The trouble is that I
can hardly remember anything that I wrote down on those tests.

I had trouble taking the information I learned for tests and applying it
in some useful way to my life. This difficulty still plagues me to this day. While
I can understand truth and see the steps to take to make it real in my life,
the process of using truth appropriately is often a challenge for me. Because
of this I am learning to evaluate my children's progress differently than tradi-
tional grades and tests do.

I want my children to be wise. I would rather they had a little information that they could utilize well than much knowledge and no clue what to do
with it. I want them to demonstrate godly character, so I observe how they

treat each other and their parents. I make corrections where necessary. I observe their personal habits and encourage them to be orderly. I watch their behavior and evaluate it in terms of what they are feeling in their hearts. Our tests are ongoing each day. There are no perfect papers. There are simply family members (me included) who by the grace of God learn more each day about how to live in a way that honors God. The final exam will come when each of us stands before Jesus, awaiting His review of how we have done in our life here on earth.

Are your children showing wisdom in their daily lives? Purpose to teach them how to *apply* information appropriately once they have learned it.

PRAYER

Lord, I confess that I haven't learned as much as I thought. I still can't seem to turn my head knowledge into heart actions. Help me to use what I know wisely. Let me be a good example for my children. Use me to be an encouragement to those around me. Please stifle my desire to know more and replace it with the ability to use what I already know more effectively. ✎

FOOD FOR THOUGHT

1. Look up the word *wisdom* in the dictionary. Does it describe the results that you are seeing in your children? If not, add some character curriculum to your lessons.

2. Role-play some situations and see how your children respond. Praise responses that reflect godly character based on wisdom. Identify weak areas for further development.

3. Spend some time in personal study of wisdom. Copy key Bible verses on note cards for a reminder of how important this is in your life.

5 0

SHE CALLED ME

The aged women likewise, that they be in behavior as becometh holiness, not false accusers, not given to much wine, teachers of good things; That they may teach the young women to be sober, to love their husbands, to love their children, to be discreet, chaste, keepers at home, good, obedient to their own husbands, that the word of God be not blasphemed.

TITUS 2:3-5

✦

What a blessing it was to hear from an older woman in our church. She was seventy years old and had raised nine children. She was blessed with over twenty grandchildren. She called me a number of times during a very busy time in my life. First she gave us bagels that she received at the end of the day from a bagel store. Then she had me over for lunch with all of my children. She remembered how few people invite large families over for a meal and wanted to make me feel special. Finally she sewed me a few nursing dresses and a couple of pairs of culottes before we moved away from the area.

This woman really ministered to me in my hour of need. Whenever I was with her, she would give me insights that the Lord had shown her. Many of these thoughts were focused on managing a large family. I left her house feeling encouraged each time. I appreciated the time she took to look after my needs. She met physical needs while sharing spiritual insights in a practical way. This was just what I needed. And to think, *she* had called me!

The biblical mandate for older women to teach younger women sure makes a lot of sense. Experience teaches so much, and maturity gives older women the wisdom to know what is truly important. I don't want to blunder through life making mistakes at every turn. The wisdom that an older woman can bring to me is of great value. Older women who make themselves available to teach younger women are precious in the sight of God.

What makes a woman "older"? There are many interpretations, but for a homeschooling mom, I believe that after you have taught your children at home for a few years and have settled into a successful routine, you have become the older woman that Titus 2 is talking about. As new moms begin homeschooling, they benefit greatly from the wisdom of the "older" moms. There is so much to learn at the beginning that it can be too much without the loving support of homeschool moms who have been there and can help. Making yourself available to new homeschool moms is a ministry of love that can have eternal significance. What a blessing for you each time you heed the call.

Do you know a new homeschool mom? Give her a call and see if there is any way you can help.

PRAYER

Lord, thank You for my friend at church. Her wisdom still touches my life even though I have moved away. Please let me be available to a woman in need as she was for me. Show me the homeschool moms who need encouragement. ⇐

FOOD FOR THOUGHT

1. Ask an older woman for her advice. They aren't always sure we value their wisdom. Nurture the relationship.

2. Be available to younger women.

3. Write a thank you note to any older women who have ministered to you.

5 1

YOU PICK THE STORE

Therefore as the church is subject unto Christ, so let the
wives be to their own husbands in every thing.

E P H E S I A N S   5 : 2 4

❧

I had a difficult time finding a new comforter and sheets when I changed the color in our bedroom. After fifteen years of blue, I wanted to go with burgundy. Since this color was popular, I figured that it would be easy to find. I looked at all of the stores that would usually have the best prices. I couldn't find anything. I looked in other stores to no avail. Finally I found just what I wanted at a very good price in a store that I had not considered. My husband had suggested the store.

At the time we were just beginning a twenty-four-hour couples' retreat at a local hotel. It seemed foolish to me to go shopping when we had a wonderful suite at the hotel. Nevertheless, I followed my husband's suggestion to look for a comforter in one particular shop. I had been to every other store. Imagine my surprise when I found just what I wanted at the lowest price I had seen. It struck me as funny, because my husband is not particularly interested in new linens. Had I insisted that we remain in the hotel, I would have missed getting the new comforter and the truth that God was showing me about my husband.

I have a problem *letting* my husband take care of me. I don't think he knows what I need. What matters to me doesn't seem to matter to him. Our timing is usually off. Many times I find it easier to take care of it myself. While it may be easier, it isn't necessarily better. If I keep fighting my husband's efforts to care for me, I am doubting God's ability to care for me through my husband. Husbands often fail to meet our needs the way we would like them to. Maybe this is just what God would have us experience for us to grow spiritually at that moment.

The Bible tells us to be subject to our husbands. It doesn't say be subject only when they are making sense. It doesn't say only when their request fits our plans. It doesn't say only when their methods are convenient for us. It simply says that wives are to be subject to their husbands. I'm glad that God saw fit to define my place so specifically. Lord willing, I will learn to stay in my place.

Do you run the show at your house? Why?

PRAYER

Father, forgive me for forgetting my place. You have placed me under the protection of my husband even when I don't feel protected. In Your infinite wisdom You have designed marriage this way. When I stop trying to run things, it seems to work better. Please help me to do a better job of letting my husband take care of me. I believe that You will work through him if I will just allow You to do so. ❧

FOOD FOR THOUGHT

1. Do you feel uncomfortable whenever you hear the biblical directive for wives to be subject to their husbands? Why? List the reasons and share these with your husband.

2. Ask your husband if he considers you a submissive wife. Be prepared for the answer.

3. Seek the Lord in prayer regarding how to apply Ephesians 5:24 to your life.

5 2

BURNED OUT

*And let us not be weary in well doing: for in due
season we shall reap, if we faint not.*

GALATIANS 6:9

I'm not sure why I deal with this annually. I start the school year enthused
with new hopes, new plans, new books. I modify our schedule, reorganize our
supplies, and hand out new pencils. By March or April I have *NO* interest in
homeschooling. It takes too much out of me. The children have cabin fever.
The plans seem old, the books are worn, and my hopes are dashed.

It's not that anything particularly bad is happening. I just don't have
anything left of me to offer—to anyone. It is right at this point that I need to
call it burnout (or whatever term you like) and switch to Plan B. Spend a
few weeks working on something completely different. *Enjoy* the children,
minimize the planning, recording, etc. This may be all that it takes to revive
a burned-out homeschool mom. If the problem does not yield to this
approach, then a consultation with my husband will help to determine what
it will take to get me back on track.

My husband sends me off to be alone as often as possible. My weariness
in homeschooling usually has to do with the number of little ones needing my
attention each day. At the moment I am about to faint, I will get my second
wind if I go off by myself for a little bit. So many times my perspective is
clouded by the intensity of my days. Even a few minutes alone will yield a
more balanced perspective that motivates me to keep on going.

It is kingdom work we are doing as homeschoolers. God will bless our efforts if we don't give up. God knows our struggles, and He knows our weaknesses. He knows when we feel as though we cannot take another minute. What a blessed place to be. When we feel that we cannot do it anymore, it gives God a chance to help us. It opens the door for the Holy Spirit to lead the lesson instead of Mom the Manager. May we be wise moms and yield it all up to the One who can and will make it work.

Have you had your fill of homeschooling? Do you want to quit?

PRAYER

Dear Lord, I need Your help. I don't know how I can make all of this happen. I am so tired. I go to bed tired, and I wake up tired. The days are so full, and I don't sit down much. I know that homeschooling is right for us, but I don't feel as if I'm going to make it. Please show me the way to put this all together properly. I need You. ⋧

FOOD FOR THOUGHT

1. Evaluate how you have handled burnout in the past. Modify your approach to this problem so that when the first signs of burnout appear, you can successfully combat it with a minimum of disruption to your family.

2. Give yourself permission to feel that you just can't do it. Then pull yourself up and seek counsel (husband first) to determine what you need most. Do whatever it takes to revive yourself.

3. Be an encouragement to other homeschoolers who are struggling. Let them know that you have struggled, too.

5 3

RENEWED BY THE WORD

All Scripture is given by inspiration of God, and is profitable for doctrine, for reproof, for correction, for instruction in righteousness.

2 TIMOTHY 3:16

God's Word is an unfailing source of spiritual renewal. Most everything that you ever need to know about anything is in that book. Principles governing our emotions, marriages, parenting, friendships, and more can be found in this work. Since this is true, it is a curious thing that I read so many other books. While other books can offer insight, practical advice, encouragement, and so much more, the Bible stands alone as the *best* source for our needs as homeschool moms.

I believe "retreats" are a good insurance policy for busy mothers. The type of retreat that I am talking about is simply getting alone. In our solitude we can then spend time in God's Word without interruption. We *need* extra time in God's Word to allow the Holy Spirit to teach us what we need to know to do our job. Think of these retreats as teacher institutes. They can be scheduled as often as needed. Failure to do so results in certain failure.

I know that I need to be reading the Bible daily. But that sounds like a routine exercise. Daily Bible reading is so much more than a routine. The Scriptures hold the answers to our daily needs, and the Holy Spirit can direct us to read just what we need for ourselves and for our family. If Scripture is indeed profitable for instruction in righteousness, then I must avail myself of these truths so I know how to train my children properly. If Scripture is profitable for correction, then I need to immerse myself in it, not only to understand how to deal with the disobedience of my children, but to understand my own need for correction.

I am humbled virtually every time I pick up my Bible and read. There is so much in there that I am not doing so well. My flaws are magnified by many of the verses. I know that I am a sinner, and it is confirmed each time I read God's Word. But it is there that I also read of how God sent His Son to earth in the form of a man to eventually die on the cross to take the punishment for *my* sins. It is through the shed blood of Jesus Christ that I am redeemed. Praise God that He inspired the Bible to teach us everything we need to know—especially how to get to heaven.

Do you read God's Word daily? Read the Bible! It renews, refreshes, and revives.

PRAYER

Father, I know that Your Word is precious and should be read by me each day, but I don't do it. Oh, I read Scripture in some way or another, but not alone where the words can pierce my soul. Show me how to make this happen every day no matter what interruptions and distractions come. If I can see to it that I get food every day, there is no reason why I shouldn't read Your Word every day, too. I'm sorry. ❧

FOOD FOR THOUGHT

1. Make yourself accountable to someone for daily Bible reading.
2. Select a Bible study to work on during your quiet time. Set a deadline for finishing it.
3. Seek God for the logistics of making this work for you.

5 4

SERVICE FOR CHILDREN

Servants, be obedient to them that are your masters according to
the flesh, with fear and trembling, in singleness of your heart,
as unto Christ; Not with eyeservice, as menpleasers;
but as the servants of Christ, doing the will of God
from the heart; with good will doing service,
as to the Lord, and not to men.

EPHESIANS 6:5-7

There sure is a lot of work to do in our home. I could not do it myself, and that is fine because I *should* not do all of the work. It is a priceless lesson in life skills for a child to be required to perform work regularly in the home. If handled properly, tasks that are performed can be an excellent opportunity to teach the joy of serving.

Some time ago we abandoned the word *chore* at our house. It was too negative and did not foster the attitude toward work that I was looking for. We began to refer to tasks as "service." Serving others does not come naturally for most of us, and I had hoped that this change in terms would help to motivate the children to be positive about their work. The results exceeded my expectations.

At times my children will bicker over who gets to perform a certain task. They both want to help. Many times my children will offer to help out with something without being asked. Often we all pitch in to take care of a job, and we get it done quickly. While it does not always work so smoothly, much of the time we see work getting done with the cooperation of the children. They help each other frequently. Good attitudes are behind the successful work ethic in our home.

While our children are taught that they must obey us, they are also learning that obedience is their act of service. When they have an attitude of serving others, the task takes on less meaning, and the giving of themselves in service becomes more important. This is so critical in the way we all respond to what the Lord would have us do. How beneficial for our children to learn how to serve the Lord through working in the home. What a blessing it is to have the opportunity to involve the children throughout the day in ways that serve others in the context of daily work in the home.

Do your children have daily responsibilities? Are these a joy to perform, or are they a burden?

PRAYER

Lord, thank You for allowing me to have more work than I can manage. I have been forced to include my children in this work, which is Your best for them in the first place. Help me to instill in them a heart motive of service in all they do each day. Remind me to praise them more often, not only for work well done but also for good attitudes. I desire to encourage their willingness to work in ways that will make it natural to serve You when they are older. Help me to be faithful to this task. ❧

FOOD FOR THOUGHT

1. Examine your attitude toward work. Is it encouraging your children?
2. Study the meaning of the word *service*.
3. Apply Ephesians 6:5-7 to the chores that need to be performed in your home.

5 5

ACTIVELY INVOLVED IN
RELATIONSHIPS

And when Jesus came to the place, he looked up, and saw him,
and said unto him, Zaccheus, make haste, and come down;
for to-day I must abide at thy house.

LUKE 19:5

❧

*A*s a homeschool mom I struggle with knowing the balance between activities and relationships. I'm not always sure what is most important. Field trips and organized activities are pretty easy to find in support groups for homeschoolers. I have not been drawn to sign my children up for a lot of these activities. It is not only because of the logistics of keeping track of many small children. I prefer to build lasting relationships through these outings, and it takes careful selection to choose those that will achieve this end.

It is good to have fun. Having fun with other homeschool families is even better. There are times when our family has become close to another family. This has not occurred during activities, however. Children can be at a field trip such as roller skating or visiting a museum and have no meaningful dialog with another child. They may meet someone they would like to get to know better, but they won't be able to do this too well during the activity. Getting together at another time can facilitate a new friendship.

Learning to build and maintain relationships with others is a life skill that will serve your children in all that they do. Adult relationships can be superficial, and I wonder if we are encouraging our children in the same direction when we have too many outings instead of nurturing a friendship. Are our children learning to serve others, or are they just going out to be entertained? We like to combine hospitality with relationships. We plan to keep Friday afternoon free to have other families over to our house. In this manner we combine an activity with relationships. This is the way Jesus worked, too.

After a busy day, Jesus sought to stay in the home of Zacchaeus who was a tax collector. He ministered to the man's needs, and they got to know each other. This was the way that Jesus built relationships. He talked with people and visited them. He did not play alongside them; he interacted with them. This model serves our family when we select our outside activities. We aim to focus on those that will allow us the greatest opportunity to get to know other people.

Are you involved in too many activities? Develop your own relationship-building activities.

PRAYER

Father, thank You for showing me how to make friendships. Thank You for helping me to discern which activities will best foster these relationships. Help me to balance our outings with those times when we invite people into our home. Make me a good example to my children when it comes to developing lasting friendships. ⊷

FOOD FOR THOUGHT

1. Do you have a means of determining how to select outside activities? If not, develop criteria to help you stay focused on those activities that best foster relationships.

2. Ask your children what interests them and use their answers to help select activities. Avoid signing them up for things they may not be interested in just because these activities sound good.

3. Seek friendships with other homeschool families who have children the ages of your own. Create your own field trip.

5 6

A TIME FOR ORDER

*Order my steps in thy word: and let not any
iniquity have dominion over me.*

PSALM 119:133

᳄

I feel that I am constantly in the process of getting organized. Just when one area is doing well, another one slides. Some days my systems all fall apart, and my home is chaotic. I don't thrive on these days. The children do not perform well in disorder, and I feel stressed when there is no program to follow. I have learned that maintaining my routine is so important that I make every effort to stay on our plan.

How you order your day is not as important as the fact that you do. Even moms with days that appear unplanned often have an outline they are following. Some people need a rigid structure while others thrive on a loosely thought-through plan. Neither approach is wrong; they are just different, as you and I are different. I like to define my day by the clock. Get up, eat breakfast, start school, and so on at a certain time each day. This establishes a routine that the children can expect. There are many interruptions to our routine that make it tough to stay on our time plan. I use certain times of the day such as mealtimes, nap times, and bedtimes as checkpoints to redirect us if needed. Some days we abandon our regular plan in favor of God's better alternative for that day. We return to our routine as soon as possible.

The physical realm is probably the easiest to order. That is where most of us put our focus. We organize our homes, our books, our day. We expend so much energy on these areas that we don't have anything left to address the other areas. The verse in Psalm 119 refers to ordering your steps in God's Word. The Bible is the key to ordering your life. It guides how you think, how you act, and what you deem important. Although it may seem easier to order the physical realm first, ordering your life through application of biblical principles will make ordering your home go more smoothly.

Chaos and confusion make for a long school day. They steal the joy from the day and rob the children of important life-skill training. God desires for us to have order in our lives and in our children's lives.

How orderly is your life? Do you need to set up a new plan?

PRAYER

Father, I confess that I spend too much time ordering my household. It is important, but not as important as first focusing on ordering my life from the truths found in Your Word. Help me to see the areas in my life that need to be changed. Show me the things that I need to teach my children regarding order in their lives. Let me never grow weary of the ongoing process of ordering my life. May my decisions in this area bring glory and honor to You. ❧

FOOD FOR THOUGHT

1. If you need to improve on your household organization, read *The Busy Mom's Guide to Simple Living.*
2. Are your children learning to organize themselves? Teach them how to be orderly.
3. Praise God for providing us a blueprint for ordering our lives in the Bible.

5 7

BONE-TIRED

He giveth power to the faint; and to them that have no might he increaseth strength. Even the youths shall faint and be weary, and the young men shall utterly fall: But they that wait upon the Lord shall renew their strength; they shall mount up with wings as eagles; they shall run, and not be weary; and they shall walk, and not faint.

ISAIAH 40:29-31

❧

There have been days when I have great plans, but wake up tired and have no energy. It frustrates me because the children are all set to go, but their teacher is not up to it. While a passive curriculum for that day works fine, my children are active and thrive on school days where I have planned some action. I try to eat well, get enough sleep, exercise, and keep my energy level up in any way that I can. Even so, it doesn't match the energy of my children.

Sometimes I feel guilty about this. I wonder if there isn't some better way to boost my potential as an energized mom. I have tried vitamins, a green drink, etc. Nothing gives me what I really want. I'll be tired forever, it seems. The Bible confirms that indeed I will have times of weariness, but notice who else experiences this same condition: "Even the youths shall faint and be weary . . ." Wow! What a concept. It isn't just a middle-aged woman like me who gets tired.

This realization gives great freedom to me as a homeschool mom. There is nothing wrong with me when I feel weak and unable to complete my plans. It comes with the territory. When you set out to undertake a demanding project, it is understood that the project will take a lot out of you. It isn't through my own efforts at becoming more energized that I will have more strength.

It is when I wait on the Lord that *He* will renew my strength. What a joy to know that it is God who gives me overcoming strength. I must wait upon Him to do this. This means that I must rest in expectation of what He promises. That is, He will renew my strength when I rest and let Him do so. This is the opposite of the way I usually work. I want to do something myself to improve my circumstances. He says to simply wait, and He will lift me up. I know I can trust God's Word because it is true. That means that even though I am tired, there is hope that I will have energy again.

Are you trying to get yourself going? Make sure you ask God to revive you.

PRAYER

Father, forgive me for complaining when I don't have the strength to follow what I have planned. Help me to see what Your best is for me each day and to allow You to strengthen me for the work of that day. Show me the balance between taking good care of myself and looking to You for strength. Thank You for being there for me. ❧

FOOD FOR THOUGHT

1. Memorize Isaiah 40:31.
2. Do you know someone who is exhausted? Visit that person and share what you have learned today as an encouragement.
3. Which gives more strength, physical exercise or spiritual exercise?

5 8

PLEASE FORGIVE ME

*Forbearing one another, and forgiving one another, if any man have
a quarrel against any: even as Christ forgave you, so also do ye.*

COLOSSIANS 3:13

It is humbling to have your children at home with you all day. They see all
of your flaws. They are on the receiving end when you sin with your mouth.
They know right from wrong because you have taught them by example.
They know when you have done something wrong. Just how effectively you
use your mistakes as a teaching tool is up to you.

It has taken some time for me to become comfortable saying "I'm sorry"
to my children. I don't say it as often as I need to, but I am learning. It might
be impatience with their careless work or a sharp word spoken in haste—
whatever my sin, I must ask them to forgive me. This isn't easy, but it is the
best way. My biblical response in a situation where I have sinned against them
is a good way to teach them by example. If I respond in an ungodly way, my
example is just as powerful even though it is negative.

It takes clarity of thought to take personal responsibility for our actions.
I still find myself trying to excuse some wrong attitudes or behaviors because
of extenuating circumstances. If this is true for me, then I am teaching my
children to sin as long as they have a good reason. We must not make this
mistake. Sin is bad all of the time. Forgiveness is good all of the time. It is
God's way.

Why is it that we can't get these simple truths applied well in our lives
and in the lives of our children? It may be pride. Pride prevents us from

saying that we were wrong. Pride blames the other person or the circumstances. Pride circumvents the biblical mandate that we forgive others as Christ forgave us.

Have you sinned against your children (or your husband) without asking their forgiveness? Deal with this matter now.

PRAYER

Lord, this is a tough subject for me to think about. I don't do so well at asking for forgiveness because sometimes I don't take personal responsibility for my own actions. I make excuses and blame others for those things that I have done wrong. Pride prevents me from modeling an appropriate response to sin for my children. Help me to get this right. I want them to become comfortable asking others to forgive them when they sin. I don't want this area to be a stumbling block to them as it has been for me. ❦

FOOD FOR THOUGHT

1. To whom do you have the most trouble saying "I'm sorry" when you are in the wrong? Try to understand why this is true and change it.

2. Are there any persons in your life who regularly humble themselves when they sin against others? Observe them closely and perhaps pick up some pointers.

3. Meditate upon the reasons why Jesus Christ died upon the cross. His death took the punishment for our sins. It is only because of Christ's sacrifice that our sins can be forgiven. If Christ did this for us, can't we forgive others? The Bible requires that we do.

5 9

DISTRACTED BY TOO MUCH

Prove all things; hold fast that which is good.

1 THESSALONIANS 5:21

❧

There is little distinction in our day between what is good and what is bad. Some would have us believe that bad things really are good. It gets very confusing to try to decide whether to do something or to have something when the criteria are fuzzy. As a result many of us have too much, and we are distracted by what we have.

All that we have in our homes can become a distraction—too much curriculum, too many supplies, too many crayons. Clothing that overflows the dresser or shoes spilling out of the closet distract us. By always wanting more and then having more, we chip away at the quality of life.

In our home, we have a goal to buy the minimum that we need to get the job done. We don't always meet our goal, but we have noticed blessings in the areas where we have minimized what we get. On the other hand, we have experienced the maintenance required when we have more than we need.

My husband isn't much for vast assortments of toys. He would prefer that we keep our toy inventory to a minimum. As we have had more children, we have needed fewer toys. We still seem to have many pieces that get separated from various toys. It was quite a visual for me when we moved to see my husband working with the boys unpacking the toys. They spent a long time trying to put the right pieces together with the right toy. It was a lot of work, and it made me think about keeping only the best and getting rid of the rest. We would then not be so distracted by the stuff that doesn't serve a useful purpose.

I so enjoy Scripture that tells me exactly what to do. To "prove all things" is pretty clear. Test everything. Make sure you "hold fast to that which is good." Don't keep things that are not good. Evaluate what you have and determine if what was good in the past is still good. If not, get rid of it. Give it to someone who can use it.

Do you test everything to be sure it is good before you commit to doing it or owning it? It would be a good policy to do so.

PRAYER

Lord, I understand that all that I have comes from You. I am grateful that You have allowed me to have so much. Help me to let go of some things to share with others. Show me which things aren't so good for me anymore. What could I give to someone else who could benefit more from it than I do? I thought I was minimizing clutter, but so many things still distract me. Teach me to look at possessions the way You do as I decide what is appropriate. ❧

FOOD FOR THOUGHT

1. Why is materialism such a great distraction?
2. Look at your schoolbooks and supplies. Are there books and materials that no longer benefit your children? Move them along to someone else.
3. Try this experiment. Do without something you think you need in a specific area. Did everything work out fine anyway? What would happen if you did this in other areas, too?

6 0

WHY ARE THEY DOING THAT?

Judge not, that ye be not judged. For with what judgment ye judge,
ye shall be judged: and with what measure ye mete,
it shall be measured to you again.

MATTHEW 7:1-2

❧

A few years back I read something about a prominent homeschooling family who hired a woman to come to their home and clean it. I was baffled because this family had a number of older daughters, and although it was a large family, I couldn't understand why they could not clean their own house. At the time this was just a passing thought, but I realize now that it was much more. I was judging this family in their decision to hire a housekeeper. Since my own daughters helped me to keep up my own house, I figured older daughters could surely get the job done. What flawed thinking I had back then.

I now realize that this family is very active in work that God has called them to do and could not take care of everything in the home, too. I imagine it was difficult even to coordinate it all. Their contribution to homeschooling is far more important than housecleaning. For them it was an excellent choice to have someone help them in their home. For other families the decision might be different.

When we see others who are struggling with maintaining a schedule, organizing their materials, keeping their homes neat, etc., we should pray for them—not criticize. The flesh immediately criticizes and voices an opinion. People don't need our criticism. They need us to be intercessors for them.

Our advice won't necessarily accomplish anything. Our prayers will help them the most. It is only by the grace of God that *we* are not experiencing the same difficulties. Someday we may find ourselves in exactly the same position as the family we are criticizing.

My life is quite full now. We have about the same number of children as this family did when they hired a housekeeper. Our own family ministry is much smaller than theirs; yet even with the help of my girls, I struggle to keep up with the work in our home. I understand now why they hired help. The husband was taking good care of his wife by doing this for her. I am ashamed that I judged them because now I see the value in what they did. While my opinion was wrong, just having an opinion in this situation at all was wrong on my part. I hope that others will pray for me when they see a need rather than pass judgment as I did on this family.

Is someone you know doing something that makes no sense to you? Praise God for diversity.

PRAYER

Heavenly Father, I am sorry that my behavior has grieved You. I know that Your plan for each of our families is different, and yet I still don't remember to appreciate this when others make decisions that I don't understand. Forgive me for thinking that I should even have an opinion about something that is not my business. ❧

FOOD FOR THOUGHT

1. How do you feel when someone judges what you are doing? Remember this when you are tempted to judge someone else.

2. Why has God made homeschooling families similar but with distinct differences?

3. Pray for those who are struggling. Don't evaluate why they are having problems; just pray that God will help them.

61

I NEED HELP!

Bear ye one another's burdens, and so fulfil the law of Christ.

GALATIANS 6:2

❦

*M*y husband was out of town for a week when I was seven months pregnant and just recovering from the stomach flu. It was more than I could bear. I needed help. I would have appreciated someone coming alongside me to bear my burden. The trouble was that I didn't tell anyone of my need. Instead, the six children and I muddled through the week, barely able to manage the minute-to-minute needs of our young family.

Before my husband left on his trip, a friend from church had mentioned that she could pick up some of the children to give me a break if I needed it. I never took her up on it. Why? Did I want everyone to think I could handle it? Was I too embarrassed to ask for help? My pride became an additional burden to us during a very demanding week.

I like to help others in need. The Lord is pleased, and I feel a satisfaction in knowing that I was able to ease the burden for someone else. But the verse also implies that there are times when I will be on the receiving end. My gracious acceptance of help offered is a blessing to those who are trying to help me. By refusing help and stubbornly doing it myself, I am depriving other people of the opportunity to follow the mandate in Galatians 6:2.

Some women have a radar for other women in need. They show up on your doorstep with just what you need the moment you need it. Most of us are not like that. If we are made aware of a need, we can meet it. Otherwise we may not know what to do. It is wise for us to make our needs known to others. Particularly when times are tough, it is good to allow others to minister to our needs. Our pride that assures everyone that we can manage must fall away and be replaced by the humility that will accept help.

Do you need some help? Let someone know today.

PRAYER

Lord, I confess that I like to handle things myself. I don't want anyone to think I can't take care of everything. I don't want to appear a failure. By not asking for help (or graciously receiving it when it comes), I am trying to show others that I can manage what is before me. The trouble is that this just isn't true, and my pride gets in the way of admitting this. Please help me to see the truth. Help me to see that it is Your plan for others to bear my burdens with me. You have set it up that way. Show me how to accept help as eagerly as I offer help. Thank You for the people who have tried to help me. ❧

FOOD FOR THOUGHT

1. Do you have a difficult time accepting help from others? Think about why this is true and determine what you need to change.

2. Do you eagerly accept the opportunities to bear the burdens of others with them? In what new ways can you be a blessing to another woman in need? Make this a priority.

3. Reflect on the people who have helped you in your hour of need. Pray for them. They may need help now.

6 2

THIS IS HEAVY

Come unto me, all ye that labor and are heavy laden, and
I will give you rest. Take my yoke upon you, and learn of me;
for I am meek and lowly in heart: and ye shall find rest unto
your souls. For my yoke is easy, and my burden is light.

MATTHEW 11:28-30

❧

The young man, Pilgrim, in the classic *Pilgrim's Progress* begins his journey carrying many burdens. But he successfully completes his pilgrimage to the Celestial City without those burdens on his back. These are necessarily shed early in his adventure. Homeschool moms need to shed burdens too at the beginning of the journey through educating their children at home. We also must learn to stop adding burdens along the way.

During our move to our farm in the months of September and October, I got that sinking feeling that we weren't "doing school." The books were packed, the schedule disrupted, and the teacher otherwise preoccupied with the move. My plans to start our new curriculum in the fall in an orderly way abruptly changed when we suddenly found ourselves moving. The ways of the Lord are good but mysterious to those of us who try to understand His timing. While excited to be finally moving to the country, I began to add burdens to the move by not releasing all of my expectations as to what "school" should look like.

I became self-reliant instead of God-reliant as I tried to decide what the children should do to occupy themselves during this disruption to our routine. My husband came up with a great plan. If only I had seen it as being enough. Older children tutored younger children in basic skills for an hour in the morning. We bought books on goats, sheep, chickens, orchards, and more. My husband had each of the older children pick a topic to research to help us get a head start on what we would do the following spring.

My ten-year-old, Jenny, selected a shepherding dog book. It was a concise presentation of the different breeds known for their working qualities. She made phone calls and wrote letters requesting information. We received a helpful magazine on border collies and located a couple of breeders in our area. She developed several skills during this project, and we benefited in a practical way from the assignment. We most certainly were "doing school" and, in some respects, doing it better than we had in the past.

Are you adding burdens to your life by your expectations of how your school should look? What does God desire for your school? Ask Him.

PRAYER

Father, I need Your guidance daily to know what I should be doing. I am not as flexible to changing circumstances as I need to be. I add unnecessary burdens. Your yoke is easy, and Your burden is light. Help me to understand this in a practical way in my daily life. ❧

FOOD FOR THOUGHT

1. In what areas of educating your children at home do you make things more difficult than they need to be? Seek the Lord's wisdom as to what ways to change.
2. Seek the counsel of more experienced homeschool moms regarding what is really important.
3. Memorize Matthew 11:30 and claim it for your school.

6 3

SHOW ME

By faith Abraham, when he was called to go out into a place
which he should after receive for an inheritance, obeyed;
and he went out, not knowing whither he went.

HEBREWS 11:8

ॐ

While putting together the contract on our farm purchase, I was feeling overwhelmed by the details. We were going to pay rent first before closing so we could get our belongings and all of our children moved out of our small house before we put it on the market. We could then clean our old home up and apply some paint where needed. We hoped it would show better and sell faster this way. We were setting up double house payments and committing to buy the farm without a contingency to sell our home first. This isn't the way we normally do things. It made me uncomfortable. I wanted to *see* how it would all work out. Our realtor just looked at me and said I didn't have enough faith. He was right.

There is a fine line between faith and foolishness. What I consider a step of faith might look like foolishness to someone else. What appears to be irresponsibility to another person may actually be the way the Lord has led me in faith. This is critical to understanding the different methods we employ to teach our children at home. Some moms use a rigid curriculum governed by textbooks. Others approach homeschooling more casually. There are many variations in between. Use what is best for you, but remember that other families will be called to homeschool in a different manner than you do.

Regardless of our methods, we all have the same decision to make about the outcome of our efforts.

Just as I wanted to *see* how the details of our farm purchase would work out, I want to *see* how my methods will work for my children. I want a glimpse at the final results. I want to know ahead of time what grade I will get in the course before I sign up and pay for my books. This sounds silly, but it is exactly what we do when we hesitate because we don't know how our children are going to turn out.

Faith is trusting the Lord to work out the details while giving up control of the details. I like to be in control. I enjoy guiding our family through a daily schedule. I like routine and order and consistency. The trouble is that none of these things make my faith grow if I must control them. How much better it would be to have more faith in the first place! God wants our children to turn out well more than we do. Apply biblical methods in training your children and have faith in the outcome.

Are you worried about whether your children will turn out okay? Allow God to build your faith in this area.

PRAYER

Lord, I confess that I challenge Your control over my life. I don't trust You to know what is best for me and for my family. My faith is so small. Please grant me the opportunities to increase my faith. ✒

FOOD FOR THOUGHT

1. List all of the reasons why you like to control people, situations, etc.
2. Project what the outcome would be in each of these areas if you yielded control of them to God.
3. Let go and let God.

6 4

A LIGHT IN THE DARKNESS

*And the things that thou hast heard of me among many witnesses,
the same commit thou to faithful men, who shall
be able to teach others also.*

2 TIMOTHY 2:2

❁

I have heard opponents of homeschooling say that we are depriving the public schools of the Christian influence that our children would have there. This is true, but not for the reasons they have outlined. If our children were in public school, it is uncertain whether their influence would be good or bad. It is unclear whether they would have a Christian testimony. It is not certain that children will be a Christian witness to other children in *any* school setting.

Our human bodies are plagued with the fleshly temptations that cause us to sin if we are not careful. Every small child, no matter how cute he or she is, has the capacity to sin. Children are naturally drawn by their sinful nature daily. They were born that way. Once they have come to know Jesus as their Lord and Savior, they are still frequently tempted to sin. Few kindergarten-aged children are saved, and even if they are, they are "baby" Christians. They are young and vulnerable and need the benefit of a strong Bible-teaching church to complement the training received from the parents in the home. They aren't yet ready to be a light in the darkness.

It is a curiosity to me that adults feel that children will be able to influence other children for Christ just because they are saved. I know that I became a Christian as an adult and was not able to share my faith clearly for years. I recently took a soul-winning course because after being saved for a decade, I still did not feel that I knew how to share the Gospel clearly. Our children don't know how to do so either unless we teach them.

We must train them to witness to others by sharing the Gospel clearly. Soul-winning doesn't just happen. Children need to be taught how to explain the Gospel, using Scripture. Memorization of Scripture is a vital component to successful sharing of the Gospel. We aren't against our children going out and influencing their peers for Christ. We want them to be ready to do it and to do it well. This won't happen until they are strong and prepared to teach others.

Are you expecting your children to be a good Christian example to the world? Do they know how?

PRAYER

Father, thank You for blessing me with the opportunity to teach biblical principles to my children in my home. Just as a greenhouse protects the young plants until they are strong enough to be planted outside, our home is a place of protection until the children are strong enough to share Your Gospel out in the world. Show me weak areas in each of my children where they could be influenced by evil. I want to train specifically in these areas so that You will have mighty warriors for the battle.

FOOD FOR THOUGHT

1. What is wrong with sending our children out in the world to represent Christ before they are trained properly?

2. Develop a means of evaluating your children regarding their preparedness to share the Gospel with a lost person.

3. Include training in soul-winning in your curriculum.

6 5

A BALANCED APPROACH

To every thing there is a season, and a time to
every purpose under the heaven.

ECCLESIASTES 3:1

❧

I have a hobby that I haven't been able to start yet. I know this sounds silly, but I have an interest that I can't pursue even though I keep preparing for it anyway. I have taken a class, bought materials, and dreamed of starting my hobby. I plan to make cloth dolls in the future. It is uplifting to me to think about the dolls that I will make and what nice gifts these will be for little girls. The recipients will likely be my granddaughters.

Seasons of life come and go, but while you are in them, they can be intense. Consider the mother with a two-year-old and a nursing infant (I have both right now). She is fortunate to sit down to a meal and eat without interruption. It rarely happens. Or what about the mother of older daughters who seem to be on the telephone every time Mom goes to use it? Teenagers may have your car frequently when you need to go somewhere yourself. And empty nesters have houses that are *extremely* quiet.

Each season has a purpose of its own. For me, the season of homeschooling restricts the taking on of new hobbies. It greatly reduces my free time. Homeschooling requires preparation time and well-thought-out goal-setting for my children. This takes time away from sewing, which I enjoy very much. I have been slow to learn how to garden because I haven't found the time yet to study what I need to know. I don't really know how to answer the question "What do you like to do?" because I haven't stopped long enough to consider what I like. There isn't much time.

Homeschooling can consume you if you are not careful. Every waking moment can be used wisely in this venture. If this is the case, then Mom is out of balance. There is more to Mom than homeschooling. Even in this intense season of life, there is some way to pursue something totally different. I don't know when I will make my first cloth doll. I have some curly hair, pencils for beautiful eyes, and a pattern to make a simple doll. I look at cloth dolls wherever I go. This is all I can fit in right now. But it energizes me to prepare for the day when I will have a chance to sit down and make a doll. That hope balances out the many hours I spend educating my children. It encourages me as I consider adding a cloth-doll-making study unit when my girls are a little older.

Is there something that you would like to do? Find a way to at least begin to pursue this area.

PRAYER

Heavenly Father, You are so good to me. You have given me full days of challenging moments. This season places great responsibility on me, and I thank You that You find me worthy of this work. Keep me mindful of the talents You have blessed me with and how best to use them during this time. ❧

FOOD FOR THOUGHT

1. Is your life out of balance? Determine why and take steps to change it.
2. Memorize Ecclesiastes 3:1. Remember this verse when homeschooling seems too much for you.
3. Cultivate at least one hobby/activity that you enjoy.

66

LET'S QUIT

Being confident of this very thing, that he which hath begun a good work in you will perform it until the day of Jesus Christ.

PHILIPPIANS 1:6

❧

I have a sentence that I use when I get frustrated. I am embarrassed even to share it because it should never leave my mouth. In fact, my husband has asked me not to repeat this sentence ever again. "I want to send you to public school!" There it is. Not so bad in its own right, if your family has decided on public school. For homeschooling families, this statement made in frustration doesn't accomplish anything positive. In my household it has made the children wonder what it would be like to attend public school. Usually it triggers the alarm system warning the family that Mom is on overload and can't take another thing. In a while she will regain her senses and wonder why she ever made the comment.

That's what they think anyway. I know why I said it. I didn't believe that I could make homeschooling work anymore. Sometimes I doubt that God will really follow through because I know how hard it is for my flesh to keep going when the work is great. The Bible says that I can have confidence that He will see the work to completion. I must believe and trust that it is true. There are moments when I can't even think clearly. Multiple children have multiple needs all at once, and I can't even begin to know what to do first. I wonder if I am getting the right things done first, since there will be no time later to do what is unfinished. I get to feeling that I just don't have the stamina to keep going. There is a lot to juggle—high school studies, elementary work, teaching reading, preschoolers, toddlers, and babies.

Endurance is continuing through a difficult time without yielding to the pressure. This is a time for your level of patience to grow. There are going to be times when homeschool moms just endure. It doesn't mean that the challenges will disappear; it means that we will persevere through them. God doesn't leave us during this time. He is right there with us and desires for us to succeed. He won't give up on the good work that He began in you, and you should not either.

Is homeschooling too much for you today? Take a deep breath and call on the Lord for reassurance.

PRAYER

Dear Lord, I am sorry that I let You down. Every time I threaten to send the children to public school, I am making a big mistake. It unsettles the whole family and implies that we don't believe You have called us to homeschool. Help me to remember that You are in this with me. You desire for this to work for our family more than I do. I know that You will not let me fail. Forgive my failure to take You at Your Word. ✴

FOOD FOR THOUGHT

1. Do you feel that you want to quit homeschooling? Why?
2. Memorize Philippians 1:6. Focus on it when you feel like giving up.
3. List the benefits of enduring the difficult days. Praise God for a long list.

6 7

CALLED TO COMMITMENT

*And he went a little further, and fell on his face, and prayed, saying,
O my Father, if it be possible, let this cup pass from me:
nevertheless, not as I will, but as thou wilt.*

MATTHEW 26:39

❧

*M*any people have asked me how long we plan to homeschool. They assume we will stop at junior high, high school, or college. For many, homeschooling is viewed as an experiment for a little while until the children go to "real" school. Our homeschool *is* real school and will be in session as long as there are children living in our home. It is a calling for us from the Lord to educate our children at home. We are committed to it for the long haul.

While some aspects of high school and higher-level learning are more challenging at home, this is where we feel God has called us. We have invested in equipment and materials to teach both our boys and girls what they need to know. Obstacles have to be overcome when you are following God's will for your family. Problems will arise that require creative solutions. As pioneers journeying through homeschooling for the first time, we are bound to experience some unexpected circumstances. This makes homeschooling exciting.

I did not understand the commitment the first year we homeschooled. The enthusiasm was still there. The excitement had not yet worn off. Teaching one four-year-old was pretty easy. Ten years later I understand commitment. It is sticking to the task no matter what. It is forging ahead, especially when the path is unclear. It is remembering why we are doing this in the first place. We don't homeschool because we don't like public school and can't afford Christian school. We homeschool because we are convicted that this is what God would have our family do.

Jesus prayed for relief from the painful trial that He was experiencing before His death on the cross. He knew why He had to die, but He still sought relief from the ordeal. This relief was requested only if the Father willed it for Him. God did not.

I have days when I would gladly welcome release from my conviction to homeschool. I could picture a smiling face making sandwiches for the children to eat while at school. I could eat my own lunch in peace. No matter—that is not where God has called me. His will, not my own, is all that matters. The challenges will continue to be mine unless God changes His mind about our homeschooling. I don't think He will.

Are you committed to homeschooling or just experimenting? Your answer will affect the outcome of your efforts.

PRAYER

Dear Lord, thank You for the privilege of homeschooling my children. There are so many benefits to having my children near me so much of the time. Our commitment to this task comes from You, and I ask for Your help as we continue to follow Your will. Keep me focused on why we are choosing this method of education. ◦↲

FOOD FOR THOUGHT

1. Make a list of all of the reasons that you decided to homeschool. Prioritize them in the order of importance.
2. Seek God's will in determining the direction of your school.
3. Experience the freedom to follow God's best for your own family. Celebrate the unique plan He has for you.

6 8

FOLLOW ME

My son, give me thine heart, and let thine eyes observe my ways.

PROVERBS 23:26

ঞ্চ

A short while after we purchased our first house, we bought a Samoyed puppy. We had no children, and I guess this satisfied my desire to take care of something. He was a cute bundle of white fluff when we brought him home weighing a little less than our children weighed at birth. We named him Casper. In an attempt to train him properly, we took him to an obedience class so that he would be a good pet.

He failed the class. He failed completely at learning who was boss. I never could control him, and eventually we gave him to a friend who lived in the country. By this time Casper was eleven years old and set in his ways. He did not thrive in the country, and our friend got rid of him. The cute little puppy that we brought home had turned into seventy-five pounds of stubborn animal that resisted being forced to do anything he did not want to do. He was just a dog, but our children will follow a similar path if our training misses a key element.

Casper's obedience class was 100 percent external rewards. We went through a lot of dog biscuits trying to train him. Children can also be trained using external rewards such as candy, extra dessert, car privileges, money, etc. But if there is no internal motivation from the child to follow your directions, you are in trouble. Children should *want* to follow you. There should not be a battle of the wills each time you make a request. Homeschooling will be difficult each day if this battle ensues. Children should understand that you have authority over them and that they must obey you.

The Scriptures teach parents to win the hearts of their children. When parents have a child's heart, that child will be able to observe the parents and learn from them. When we lose the heart of our child, it is difficult to teach him. He rebels and does it his own way. As homeschoolers we have a great opportunity to nurture the relationship with our child as we share our day together. Talk often about what your child is feeling and stay in touch with her concerns. Take the extra time to keep her heart now.

Do your children follow you, or do you have to coerce them to do what you ask of them? Is this satisfactory to you?

PRAYER

Dear Father, You have given me a special job of raising and training my children properly. Help me to stay close to them and know what they are feeling. Make me sensitive to their needs. Show me the best way to be in touch with them and keep their hearts. Remind me to take as much time as I need to in order to do this right. I'm glad that You have my heart. ❧

FOOD FOR THOUGHT

1. Do your children need external rewards before they will do what you have asked them to do? Restructure your reward system to eliminate some (all, if necessary) of these external rewards.

2. Do you have your children's hearts?

3. You might view a copy of Dr. S. M. Davis's video *My Son, Give Me Thine Heart* (to order call 800-500-8853).

6 9

HOME SWEET HOME

*Better is little with the fear of the Lord, than
great treasure and trouble therewith.*

PROVERBS 15:16

❧

*U*ntil recently I had only homeschooled in houses that were small and
crowded. Try as I would to utilize the space well, it just never worked very
efficiently. Many of us are one-income families who are challenged to find suit-
able housing for a family at home all day conducting school. At times the walls
crowd us in as we try to use our homes in ways for which they were not
designed.

Have you ever wondered what a home would look like that was designed
for homeschooling? Laundry room, bathroom, and kitchen located conve-
niently near the separate room for homeschooling. One central location where
all books and materials would fit would certainly be a blessing. This is not
the model home that most of us live in. Usually we have books and supplies
in various rooms, and cooking and laundry may take place far enough from
where the children are working that we find ourselves doing a lot of walking.

We looked at larger homes in our suburban location and came away
disappointed. The ones we could barely afford needed work that would take
precious time away from our family. After considering our alternatives, we
decided to be content with the small home we were in and remodel the
kitchen to make it more functional. I remember feeling a little discouraged
because I had already rearranged and redesigned the living space a few times.

I did not know how I would find a place for our seventh child once she moved into the crib. It was tight.

Through an act of the Lord, we were blessed with the opportunity to move to a ten-acre farm before we began our kitchen project. While I love our farmhouse and the outbuildings and would not trade this lifestyle for suburban living, I have had my eyes opened. There is a lot more to clean in this bigger house. Repairs and updates are needed even in our well-maintained home built in 1907. With greater treasure comes greater responsibility. I am glad for the time I lived in small houses. It enabled me to focus on God's work first—homeschooling our children.

Are you happy in your home? Thank God for it.

PRAYER

Heavenly Father, thank You for allowing me the privilege of living in tight quarters for so long. I learned many things I would not have learned any other way. Forgive me for my restless spirit that craved a larger home in the country. In Your perfect timing I did enjoy this blessing, but not a minute too soon. I am grateful that my children are old enough to help me with the added work we have in our new home. Bless those women homeschooling in small spaces. Help them to develop their skills in organizing and maximizing what they have without feeling restless as I did. You always know just what we need when we need it. Thank You for taking such good care of me. ❧

FOOD FOR THOUGHT

1. Do you long for a larger home? Have you maximized the potential in your current home?
2. List all that you could change in your home to make it easier to homeschool (example: buy a shelf).
3. Pick two items on your list and do them.

7 0

COME ON—YOU CAN DO IT!

*Therefore said he unto them, The harvest truly is great, but the
laborers are few: pray ye therefore the Lord of the harvest,
that he would send forth laborers into his harvest.*

LUKE 10:2

❧

I understand this verse better now that I live on a farm. When the time
comes to harvest the crops, it must be done quickly before they are ruined
by weather or other calamities. The work is great, and the farmer benefits
from the help that he has during the harvest. If the farmer worked alone, it
is possible that he could not manage the task by himself and would lose
some of the crops.

When it comes to sharing the Gospel with lost souls, there are few laborers compared to the many lost souls that need to hear the saving message of
Jesus. For God to send laborers into His harvest, people need to be ready
and willing to go. They need to love Jesus and be assured of their salvation.
They need to know how to share the Gospel clearly. Where do these people
come from? They can come from our homes if we take the challenge to train
children up in the way they should go.

Raising and training children for Christ is a lot of hard work. Sometimes
the workload is so heavy we are tempted to find another way to get them
trained. This is not God's way. He placed our children in our home for His
good purpose, and we had better not run from His perfect plan. If someone

had not shared the good news of Jesus with me, I would be lost and destined for hell myself.

It excites me to think that my children can be used of the Lord to win others to Christ. I have such a great opportunity to train them in my home. We can memorize Scripture, role-play witnessing to the lost, and knock on doors together. If the harvest is great and the laborers are few, then I *must* take my responsibility to train them seriously. We *can* raise up well-trained workers for the harvest. God will benefit from the souls that will be saved because our children know how to share their faith with someone else. For this reason alone it is worth every effort it takes for me to keep on going and train my children properly.

Isn't it worth it? Keep up the good work!

PRAYER

Lord, thank You for allowing me so much time with my children to teach them how to share the truth of the Gospel with others. I am still learning myself, and we can grow together in this area. Help me to memorize Scripture more quickly so that I know the verses that will help lost people to see their need of a Savior. Touch each of the hearts of my children so that they will have a burden for lost souls. Make my burden stronger. ❧

FOOD FOR THOUGHT

1. Envision the ways that your children will influence others for Christ as they get older.
2. Nurture qualities in your sons that would help them to be good preachers in case they are called.
3. Take your children soul-winning. They need to learn to do this with ease.

7 1

A GENTLE TONE OF VOICE

Let no corrupt communication proceed out of your mouth,
but that which is good to the use of edifying, that
it may minister grace unto the hearers.

EPHESIANS 4:29

❧

When I was growing up, my dad repeatedly told me, "Jackie, it isn't *what* you say but *how* you say it." I don't say things in the right tone of voice. My words can be sharp and biting. They can crush and hurt. Wise words spoken in a harsh tone miss their mark. I watch the content of my speech, but amazingly I still struggle with my tone of voice.

The tongue truly is a double-edged sword. It is used for good and for evil. I desire to keep evil to a minimum, but my tongue is probably the most sinful part of my body. When I am tired or sick, my tongue is dangerous. I say things that I normally would not say. There is an edge in my voice that should not be there. Yes, I have even been known to yell. What good is an out-of-control mother to her children?

I very much want to improve in this area, but I have had little progress because I haven't understood the role my children play in the home. They are there to be trained. If they already knew how to do things, they would not need to be trained. If their character was already developed, they would not need me. If they knew their academics, I would have no reason to home-school them. So if children are in the home to be trained, then it is wise to expect them to need correction. They will need to be reminded. They will need special instruction. They will need follow-up—a lot of follow-up. None of these needs should surprise me nor cause me to speak to them in anything but a gentle tone of voice.

I don't understand completely how to do this. This is one of my weakest areas. I do know that Ephesians 4:29 makes my path clear. The words coming out of my mouth must be good. They must be useful to edify and minister grace to my children. I will have to give account for all other words spoken. The choice is mine—either change or by my example transfer tongue problems to my children. Now this is scary. They are with me all of the time. My influence on them is great. It must be positive. My words must be kind. My speech to my family must be sweet.

Do you have sweet speech all of the time? Like me, you may need to get on your knees and ask God to forgive you.

PRAYER

Dear Father, I don't know what to say. I have really blown it in the tongue department. I let too many things provoke me. I forget that my job is to train imperfect children to do a good job. I get impatient, and then I crab at them. There is a better way—Your way. Please help me. ❧

FOOD FOR THOUGHT

1. Do you use a different tone of voice when you speak to your children than you do when you speak to a friend? Why?

2. Are your children speaking kindly to one another? Train carefully in this area.

3. Do you have sweet speech toward your husband?

7 2

SLEEP 101

Love not sleep, lest thou come to poverty: open thine eyes,
and thou shalt be satisfied with bread.

PROVERBS 20:13

✧

I would like to teach a new class in our school. It would have a limited enrollment. Only I could take the class. It would be called Sleep 101. The class would have sporadic meeting times that would occur spontaneously when I haven't had enough sleep. It would be required that I go to bed until I felt rested. This could occur anytime during the day. If I needed to sleep all day, there would be bonus points. Children would cheerfully maintain order in the home until I woke up.

Back to reality—I'm not getting enough sleep. I haven't felt well-rested in years. Various things trigger this problem. Sick children, pregnancy, nursing babies, teething babies, and my husband's fire pager going off at night are the big ones. For the most part I have learned to live with the sleep deprivation. I function pretty well in spite of it. I know a day will come when I won't have these sleep disruptions, but not anytime soon. My husband has another ten years before he can retire as a firefighter. His sleep deprivation will continue for at least that long. What a set of parents we make when we both have had interrupted sleep!

The Bible says to "love not sleep." I believe that these words can bless us as homeschool moms. We may have to stay up later at night than we would like in order to get all of our work done. We might get up earlier in the morning to get a head start on the day. We might do both and be short of sleep. The reason we are not to love sleep is that it can bring us to poverty. This means we are to work. We are to keep busy and not focus on sleep.

Sleep deprivation can wreak havoc with our health. It is good to strive for a good night's sleep. We need to give our bodies a rest. But don't be disappointed if it doesn't happen. We are working hard. We put in long hours. We are not being lazy. This is good. We are in good company. The virtuous woman described in Proverbs 31 rose early in the morning while it was yet night. Her lamp did not go out at night. She probably did not get enough sleep either. Her value was far above rubies.

Do you get enough sleep? It may be that you are working hard at God's best for you.

PRAYER

Lord, did You get enough sleep? I only remember stories in the Bible about how hard You worked. Sleep was not Your focus. It should not be mine either. Help me to cheerfully give some of mine up when You need me to do so. I pray for just enough to keep me healthy. ❧

FOOD FOR THOUGHT

1. List the problems that you encounter when you have not had enough sleep.
2. Plan in advance what your expectations will be on days when you or the children have not had enough sleep.
3. Plan early-to-bed nights each week for your family—to balance those nights when the family does not get enough sleep.

7 3

CONFIDENCE

*For the Lord shall be thy confidence, and shall
keep thy foot from being taken.*

PROVERBS 3:26

✌

*C*onfidence is a great asset to the homeschool mom. It helps her to accomplish many things in her homeschooling endeavors. It is a God-given blessing that allows her to achieve far beyond her own abilities. When we rely on the Lord, He enables us to do much more than we ever thought possible. As we recognize the Lord as our source of confidence, any pride we may have in our own abilities fades away. Your confidence, however, may be misinterpreted.

Some of the negative reactions you get regarding your homeschooling may be a result of people misunderstanding your source of confidence. The confidence that you have in what you are doing may be perceived as pride. Others who believe they could never homeschool may feel that you are thinking they are inferior to you. While this is typically not the case, the perception is there just the same. Ironically, many homeschoolers feel insecure as they begin educating at home. All of us need to draw on the Lord as our source of confidence.

Confidence that comes from our Lord is found through a right relationship with Him. We must ask Jesus to be our Lord and Savior. We must confess our sin and repent. Repentance means doing whatever it takes to make things right. It is not saying that you are sorry and continuing to behave inappropriately. Changing sinful behavior can be difficult, particularly when we are trying to break bad habits. A right relationship with the Lord is nurtured in daily quiet devotional and prayer time. This means that we must provide this time and be faithful to it.

Often we look to externals for our source of confidence. It may be our abilities, our curriculum, our lesson plans, or many other factors. We may seek the advice of other homeschoolers. These all provide a false sense of security. It is only the Lord who can keep your foot from slipping. Only through reliance on Him do we have any confidence at all in our ability to homeschool. The next time you get a negative reaction about your homeschooling, take it as an opportunity to witness for Christ. Make it clear that with God all things are possible, and that is where you derive your confidence. Glory in those opportunities to share Jesus with someone who does not know Him.

Are you sure you can homeschool? Draw on the Lord for your confidence.

PRAYER

Father, thank You for the journey through homeschooling. I am way beyond being able to do this in my own power. Although I feel confident in what we are doing, it is a confidence that comes from You. Many a time You have kept Your word and kept my foot from slipping. You have given me the courage to press on when I thought I could not do it. Thank You for showing me my own insufficiency. I am grateful that You are my confidence. ❧

FOOD FOR THOUGHT

1. Do you feel insecure being the primary teacher of your children? Why?
2. Is your relationship with Jesus Christ a personal one where you draw on Him for your confidence?
3. Make a list of steps to take to improve upon your relationship to Christ.

7 4

TIME OFF

Redeeming the time, because the days are evil.

EPHESIANS 5:16

✣

*B*eekeeping is fascinating. There are so many good lessons to be learned from the bees. The queen bee encourages me to keep to our schedule. She does not lay eggs over the winter because it would demand too much from the hive during the dormant season. She follows her instinct to lay or not to lay eggs at the proper time. If I follow my instinct to adhere to a rigid schedule or to be more flexible for a period of time, I find that our schooling goes much better.

There was a woman at a church that I attended who gave birth to a Down's syndrome boy. She homeschooled and had some decisions to make regarding the use of her time. She flew across the country to speak with a specialist who trained her to stimulate her son so that he would achieve his greatest potential. These exercises took hours each day and forced a new schedule upon them. This wise mother knew that she needed to devote this time to her son in his infancy. Other plans needed to be shelved or postponed.

Wouldn't it be helpful if we could evaluate our days without waiting for a hardship to come along and wake us up? Children who are not feeling well, unexpected company, and special opportunities are examples of times to reevaluate our plans and modify if necessary. For a long time when we began homeschooling, I felt obligated to follow my plan no matter what. There were some discouraging moments as I tried to stick to my order of things when the Lord had something better for us. There are many *good* things that keep us from doing God's *best* for our family. It is vital that we redeem the time.

Don't feel guilty when you change the schedule. I have found my fears about not following the lesson plans for an extended time unwarranted. Once we resume our regular schedule, I am always amazed at how quickly we cover the material. We have experienced adjusted schedules during pregnancy and moving to a new home, as well as at other times. While it is uncomfortable for me to conduct school in a more relaxed fashion, it is what is required of me from time to time.

Do you need to modify or completely redo your schedule? Take a few days off to evaluate what needs to be changed and take up your new schedule with renewed enthusiasm.

PRAYER

Heavenly Father, I struggle with modifications to my plans. It makes me uncomfortable when I can't follow our schedule. I add much stress to my life when I fail to acknowledge the many interruptions that You bring to me for my own good. Make me more flexible to set aside the good to make room for Your best. Let me be discerning when it comes to my daily plans. ❧

FOOD FOR THOUGHT

1. Do you find it difficult to deviate from your plans? What if something better comes along for that day?
2. How do you decide what is best for your family each day? Seek God's will daily.
3. Praise God for allowing you to grow in flexibility.

7 5

I NEED SUPPORT

This know also, that in the last days perilous times shall come.
For men shall be lovers of their own selves, covetous, boasters,
proud, blasphemers, disobedient to parents, unthankful, unholy,
without natural affection, trucebreakers, false accusers,
incontinent, fierce, despisers of those that are good.

2 TIMOTHY 3:1-3

I have noticed that in certain circles homeschooling is not very popular. It does in fact incite some people to behave foolishly as they tell you how bad homeschooling is for your children. They believe our children are growing up deprived. The Bible clearly states that in the last days there will be those who despise those that are good. As we follow what God has called us to do regarding education for our children, we have experienced some fierce attacks for our decision to homeschool. Homeschooling works and is good, and I believe that attacks will continue, if not intensify, throughout our years as homeschoolers.

Because we are doing something nontraditional, we are easily misunderstood. Feelings get hurt as teachers take it personally that we don't think they are good enough to teach our children. Church members may become suspicious if we decide not to participate in Sunday school, Awana, or other organized meetings. The truth is that there are so many varied reasons why homeschoolers do what they do that nobody can accurately guess the motives behind any of it. This hostility makes for a very lonely experience unless there is a means of support.

In a culture that makes raising godly families challenging, we need supportive elements. We receive mail from organizations that work to preserve our freedoms to homeschool in our state. We help them financially. We fellowship with other homeschoolers who understand what we are doing. Iron sharpens iron during many of our visits with like-minded families. Our church is pro-family. Every single message encourages me in some way as I work to nurture my family. Our pastor homeschools and preaches homeschooling as a desirable educational option.

At this time I feel quite supported in my work as a homeschool mom, but that has not been the case much of the time. I have not been surrounded by godly homeschool families. I haven't been in such a supportive church environment. There is certain to be a good reason for this lack of support. I question my need to be surrounded by people who support me. If God freely gives us what we need, then He has already given me enough support. People can be a blessing to me, but not nearly the blessing that I receive in the person of Jesus Christ.

Are you seeking after people to be a support to you? Have you been seeking Christ first?

PRAYER

Father, forgive me for looking to people to meet my deepest needs. You know that I need support, and You are there for me. When I look to other people first, I miss the tremendous blessing available to me through You. Thank You for understanding my needs better than anyone else could. ❧

FOOD FOR THOUGHT

1. What is it about the support of others that we crave the most? Approval?
2. In what ways does Jesus support us? (Example: someone who hears our prayers and understands our needs.)
3. How can we be supportive of other homeschoolers?

But You Said You Would Do It!

*But whoso keepeth his word, in him verily is the love of God
perfected: hereby know we that we are in him.*

1 JOHN 2:5

༔

*J*immy and Jonathan walked up looking sad. "Mom, you made pregnance
[*sic*] tea again. You promised when you finished the pitcher, you would
make regular iced tea." It was true. I was in such a routine of making another
pitcher of pregnancy herbal tea that I forgot that I had promised the boys I
would make the iced tea they liked. It seems so insignificant, but it really
was important to them. More significant was my failure to follow through
on what I said I would do.

I had let the boys down and had given them reason to doubt my word
in the future. This can happen in so many areas of our school that it makes
me uncomfortable to think about it. How many times have I indicated that we
would take this or that field trip, but we don't ever get to it? How often do I
mention a particular activity without planning a way to take part in it? You
can call this disorganization or poor planning, but it is more severe in terms
of results.

Once we allow ourselves to make commitments to our children that we
don't keep, we are in trouble in a couple of ways. They view our example as
a good excuse to fail to keep their own word. It doesn't take much for this to
become lying. Now we are dealing with sin. Our poor example doesn't say

much for the influence of Christ in our own lives. Our testimony is negatively affected by failing to keep our word. Our dependability is questionable.

My boys have long forgotten that I did not make them iced tea. But they don't forget whether they can count on their mother to do what she says. If they can count on my word to be true, how much easier it will be for them to see that God's Word is true. If I profess to be something other than what I am, it makes it more difficult for them to believe that Christ was who He said He was. Keeping your word to your children has profound impact on their lives. It is a serious matter.

Have you done what you told your children you would do today? Get it done!

PRAYER

Father, I confess to You that I have a bad habit of making statements aloud to my children that I do not follow through. Although the children forgive me, I know that I am teaching them to doubt the sincerity of my words. Let this not be so any longer. Help me to learn to make fewer commitments ahead of time until I am sure we can do what I say we will do. Help me to be more spontaneous. Keep me from overcommitting, which further complicates this problem.

FOOD FOR THOUGHT

1. How do you feel when people say they will do something, but they never do it?

2. Do you frequently do this to your children?

3. Commit to nothing unless you are quite sure you will do it. It is better to announce something at the last minute than to say something in advance that you don't get around to doing.

7 7

WHERE IS MY TREASURE?

*Lay not up for yourselves treasures upon earth, where moth and
rust doth corrupt, and where thieves break through and steal: But
lay up for yourselves treasures in heaven, where neither moth nor
rust doth corrupt, and where thieves do not break through nor steal:
For where your treasure is, there will your heart be also.*

MATTHEW 6:19-21

In a materialistic culture it is obvious where people put their attention.
They spend much time acquiring and maintaining their things. Material
goods that are treasured take time and money to accumulate. They require
space to store. Ultimately, our earthly possessions will not be ours any longer
when we go to heaven. In the meantime they may be destroyed, lost, or stolen.
Eternal treasures don't come to such an end. They last forever and warrant our
diligence in storing them up.

Educating our children at home takes much of our time. There are many
opportunities that we must forgo in order to homeschool. I wish that I could
take a class, learn to quilt, or spend more time reading. Working part time
could provide materially for our family in the areas of clothing, housing,
furniture, and vacations. None of these pursuits are really very important to
me, though, because they aren't where my heart is.

My treasures are my children. I'm not sure I fully comprehend what
that means yet. I know that by homeschooling them, I am having a significant
impact on their development. I have limitless opportunity to teach them

biblical truth. I can detect weak areas and help these to be corrected before they are a big problem. There is so much that I can do because they are with me all day long. What I haven't really understood yet is the impact this will have on my grandchildren.

I have seven children, and if these seven have seven of their own, I will have forty-nine grandchildren. If these grandchildren are taught the ways of the Lord and are saved by God's grace, they will influence many others for the cause of Christ. There is no earthly possession worth more than the souls of my children and grandchildren. If I am pursuing earthly goods, it takes time away from training my children. The salvation of my children and their children and their children after them is worth more than I can put a price tag on. My children are my treasures, and that is where I put my heart.

Where is your heart? Value what God values.

PRAYER

Heavenly Father, You showed me long ago the futility of reaching for the material goods of this world. Thank You that my "stuff" has no grip on me. While I acknowledge this truth, help me to further develop my commitment to training my children to follow Jesus. Show me each day how to influence them for Christ. Bless my grandchildren by the way their parents were trained. Thank You for giving me this opportunity to value my children as You value them. ✌

FOOD FOR THOUGHT

1. What material goods do you treasure? Are these more important to you than your children?
2. How do your lifestyle choices (where you spend your time and money) reflect where your heart is?
3. Make changes to your lifestyle where needed.

STANDING ALONE

At my first answer no man stood with me, but all men forsook me:
I pray God that it may not be laid to their charge. Notwithstanding
the Lord stood with me, and strengthened me; that by me the preaching
might be fully known, and that all the Gentiles might hear: and
I was delivered out of the mouth of the lion.

2 TIMOTHY 4:16-17

I remember the enthusiasm I had as a new homeschooler. It was exciting to me to embark on such a novel approach to educating our children. There were so many benefits, and I eagerly anticipated the days ahead as we had school at home. It was surprising to me that many people did not share this enthusiasm. Neighbors, friends, and family questioned our plans. Many were skeptical. None of them were cheerleaders for us. We were on our own.

I struggle with being different. I like to "fit in." I tire of feeling as though I need to prove myself to others who do not understand homeschooling. There are also those who understand it and are dead set against it. Each time I come in contact with these people, it reminds me that we are standing alone. Over the years we have developed friendships with other homeschooling families. Some of these relationships are long distance and yet are still close as we spend time on the telephone. Other friendships are at church, which provides weekly fellowship with people who support homeschooling. Daily living, however, often entails standing alone.

Paul experienced times of standing alone. At a preliminary hearing before a trial, Paul found himself without a single advocate. Everyone had deserted him. His circumstances were surprisingly similar to our own. He was living in an anti-Christian environment, and his uncompromising, outspoken nature was too much for even his friends. The way he handled the rejection of his friends is an excellent model for us. Paul expressed an understanding of their abandonment and wished that it not be held against them.

We do well to look on those who misunderstand and reject us in just the same manner. Don't hold it against those who do not support you. Don't bemoan the lack of support from your family. There is one far more important who supports us completely. We can depend on God, just as Paul did, for our strength. Our enthusiasm for homeschooling need not wane just because those around us are not for it. Our strength comes from the Lord who gives us what we need to be able to stand alone.

Are you standing alone? You are in good company.

PRAYER

Lord, I confess that I seek the approval of people. I want people to like me and approve of what I am doing. I like cheerleaders. I want others to be for my cause. Forgive me for placing my focus in the wrong place. It is You I am pleasing and no other. Thank You for giving me the chance to homeschool and to please You in the way I do it. ⊰

FOOD FOR THOUGHT

1. Do you know how to stand alone? Ask the Lord to teach you.
2. Do you seek the approval of man? Choose something better. Seek the approval of God.
3. Are you teaching your children how to stand alone? They need to know how.

79

LITTLE ONES

But Jesus called them unto him, and said, Suffer little children to
come unto me, and forbid them not: for of such is the kingdom of God.

LUKE 18:16

There are times when I like to go grocery shopping by myself. It is a chance
for me to be alone and gather my thoughts. One afternoon I was planning
such a trip to the store when my three-year-old Joanna came down the stairs
and announced that she wanted to go "grocering" with me. She had put her
sandals on and was all ready to go. I could hardly say no. She came with
me, and I enjoyed watching her push the child-sized cart in the store. She
even reminded me to buy catsup. We had a very enjoyable special time
together.

So often Joanna is the one who gets lost in the shuffle. The busy day
ends before we read a story or play a game. Even though my younger children
are with me all day, it is easy for them to tag along without ever having meaningful interaction with Mom. Teaching the older children, preparing meals,
conquering the mountain of laundry, and much more crowd out that special
time with our young children if we are not careful.

We are very busy, but then so was Jesus. When people were bringing
little children to Him, His disciples were not pleased. They must have thought
that Jesus had more important things to do. Maybe they thought that children
were just getting in the way of His ministry. Possibly the disciples wanted to
protect Jesus from anything that might take too much of His time. The disciples may have looked at the children as an interruption.

Jesus had the right response to the little children. He made time for them. They were important to Him. He demonstrated their value by letting them come to Him. He didn't merely say they were important; He showed them they were. Jesus was a busy man. He made time. So must I. Small children can easily get lost in our homeschool. They need to be a part of our school. They need to sit on our laps and be right in the middle of what is going on. It won't always be convenient. It may not be easy. It doesn't matter. Children are our ministry.

Have you spent quality time with your little ones today? Do it!

PRAYER

Heavenly Father, I feel like a failure. So many times my little ones, especially Joanna, have come to me for something, and I was too busy. I did not take time for them. I did not give them what they should have had. I put something of lesser value ahead of them. Help me to get balanced so that I can get my other work done in less time. Show me shortcuts in the daily routine that will give me more special time with the little ones. Give me a love for playing games with the children. Help me to make this a priority. ❧

FOOD FOR THOUGHT

1. Do you have a child who needs more attention? Commit yourself today to providing what this child needs.
2. If Jesus was not too busy for the little ones, can we afford to be too busy?
3. Make a "date" to do something special alone with each of your children.

8 0

I LOVE YOU, BROTHER

Be kindly affectioned one to another with brotherly love;
in honor preferring one another.

ROMANS 12:10

෯

*J*amie was turning twelve, and Jonathan (age five) wanted to get her a gift. This was entirely his own idea, and I decided to take him out to look for the perfect gift. Jonathan was in touch with what his sister would like. He selected a bouquet of flowers, and after some deliberation, chose a beautiful birthday card depicting a teapot and teacups. He knew how to make his sister happy.

This same son on another day has the potential to make his sister very upset. Jonathan can aggravate his siblings effectively without much effort. He can be unkind. He did not need to be taught how to do this. It came naturally. For him, knowing how to please his siblings also comes naturally. He has a sense of what will make other people happy. This gift could be the exception rather than the rule.

Children need to be taught how to make each other happy. They should be shown how to honor one another. Honor means value. If we value others, then we don't destroy their things. If we value others, we don't say bad things about their interests. We don't tease or make fun of their physical appearance. We respect them. These behaviors must be taught to our children. Showing love for other people is a life skill that will serve our children well beyond childhood.

Childhood bickering with one another seems inevitable. The good that can come from such a situation is determined by how you decide to handle it. Teach your children how to show love toward each other instead of being annoyed. Show them how to overlook something that might otherwise provoke them. Train them to look out for the best interests of others. Demonstrate your own commitment to loving others by your daily behavior. It is in the home that your children will learn how to behave. It is in the home that they will learn how to treat others in God's family. Let it be in your home that the children get this right.

Is your home a place where love and honor are shown? Often?

PRAYER

Father, I am not such a good example of showing honor. I don't always treat others in my family as though they have value. Kindness does not always flow from my mouth. What an example I am! Please mold me into the kind of mother who teaches her children by her good example. Let me pass over those things that would have set me off in the past. Help me to seize every opportunity to show love and honor to my husband and to my children. May our home be a place of peace. ❧

FOOD FOR THOUGHT

1. Demonstrate in specific ways how your children can show love to one another. Role-play appropriate responses to various situations. Practice responding correctly.
2. How do *you* treat others in God's family? Are you a good example?
3. Look for opportunities to turn a squabble into a chance to demonstrate love and honor. Praise your children each time they do this well.

8 1

WHAT WAS I SUPPOSED TO GET?

For God is not the author of confusion, but of peace,
as in all churches of the saints.

1 CORINTHIANS 14:33

❧

On a hot summer day our family took a trip to Wal-Mart to get a few things. I did not have a list. I figured that I would remember everything that we wanted to buy. We bought weights to build arm strength, a bicycle helmet, and pulls for the ceiling fans. I thought that we had accomplished something until we were three-quarters of the way home, and I realized that we had forgotten what we went there for in the first place—an oscillating fan. We turned around and went back to the store.

I have a lot on my mind. Too much it seems. I can't remember details like I used to. This leads to confusion. I find myself standing in a room without any idea why I am there. Certainly I was in pursuit of something, but I can't remember what. My thinking becomes clouded when I have too much on my mind. I don't make the best decisions or have enough patience during these times. Confusion leads to frustration when I have no plan to clear my head.

Homeschool moms need to be organized. We need to have orderly homes. We need to exemplify to our children how to have clarity of thought when there is much to distract us. For me this requires that I take time away from my responsibilities periodically to clear my head. Today I am going inline skating. On another day I may go to the library. It can be as brief as five minutes or as long as it takes. I know that unless I clear my head, I won't be able to handle my responsibilities well.

God is not the author of confusion. The verse above refers to the exercise of spiritual gifts in the local church. But God doesn't want confusion in our homes either. Circumstances will prevail that make order difficult, if not impossible. When we creatively overcome these difficulties, we show our children how to do the same. When we have too many thoughts in our head, the clearing of our minds models an important skill for them. What an opportunity we have to teach our children to be successful in an important area. Those who can clarify what is critical and stay calm amid confusion will bring order to the situation.

Are you confused? Too much on your mind? Take a break.

PRAYER

Lord, I confess to You that I am confused. I have so many details floating around in my head that I don't know what to do next. I forget important things. I write things down and then forget where I wrote them. I like to be organized, but I find myself in disorder. I want to honor You by having an orderly home. Please help me to keep things in line. ❧

FOOD FOR THOUGHT

1. Make a list of ten activities (example: taking a bath, reading a poem, going to the library, etc.) that you find relaxing.
2. Have someone hold you accountable to do one of these activities when you are confused.
3. Memorize 1 Corinthians 14:33. Recall this verse on days when things seem to be going out of control.

8 2

PLEASE LISTEN

He that answereth a matter before he heareth it,
it is folly and shame unto him.

PROVERBS 18:13

✍

*L*ate in the evening my oldest daughter will come into our bedroom and want to talk. Often this occurs precisely one minute or less after I open a book to read. The day has finally ended, and I have a few moments to myself before dropping off to sleep. It would be easy to brush her off and tell her that my "kid day" has ended, and we can talk later. This would be the wrong thing to do. Her concerns are important to her, and they are to me too. Exhausted or not, I *must* be available to my older children. I need to give them this uninterrupted time.

In a busy homeschooling household, it is not easy to find a quiet time to talk. Out of necessity this time may be late in the day when younger children are in bed. In order to be able to meet the emotional needs of my older children, I need to be in touch with what is going on with them. Just because we share the same house all day does not mean that I automatically know what my children are thinking and feeling. I can't successfully relate to them when I don't provide time to listen.

It would be easier to give our older children a pat answer to their concerns. It would be easier to assume that just because they are homeschooled, we are already in touch with them, we know where they are and what they are feeling. The problem is that this just isn't the case. The older ones need our time. They need our listening ear. They need to know that we care about what matters to them. They need special time away from the younger children.

I wish I knew how to get by with less sleep. The babies wake me in the middle of the night, the family needs me during the day, and my husband and the older children need private time with me in the evening. I feel stretched. I feel ill-equipped to meet all of these needs. It is only with the Lord's help that I can even begin to be what I need to be to each member of my family. The older children especially need the listening ear of a caring mother—the same type of listening ear that I have in Jesus.

Do your older children have enough private time with you? Ask them.

PRAYER

Father, my day already seems long enough. I don't see how I can make it any longer to stay up and talk when older children need to talk. But I must. I want to. I don't know how. Help me to give each one of my children as much time as he or she needs. Bless me with needing less sleep. Thank You for always listening to me. As always You are the best example. ❧

FOOD FOR THOUGHT

1. Are you available for your older children to talk with you privately? Do your children know this, or are they afraid they are bothering you?

2. As women, we often get our emotional needs met by sharing our feelings with our spouse or friend. Make sure that you are the one your teen feels comfortable with when it comes to sharing concerns.

3. Praise God for open communication.

8 3

WISE ABOUT WHAT IS GOOD

For your obedience is come abroad unto all men. I am glad therefore on your behalf: but yet I would have you wise unto that which is good, and simple concerning evil.

ROMANS 16:19

⚘

When we lived in suburban Chicago, there was a popular drug-awareness program in the public schools. The intention of the program was to educate children about the hazards of drugs so they would stay away from them. The problem was that after some time, the program had failed to demonstrate that it decreased drug use. The statistics reflected no change, and the people who started the program were disappointed in these results.

A simple biblical truth was violated by this drug-awareness program. Rather than keeping the children simple concerning evil, the program taught the children all about evil. While the intentions of the program were honorable, the methods were not. If we wish the best for our children, then we must teach them the best. If we desire for them to flee evil, we must not expose them to evil. Evil was a strong temptation for many a fallen saint. How much more dangerous it is for our children.

Our practice of keeping our children with us except for selected controlled circumstances has been met with raised eyebrows. The public becomes concerned that our children are missing something by being "sheltered" so much. Praise God for the evil they are missing. By keeping our children in close proximity to us, we know what they are being exposed to and how they are handling it. We can observe them as they interact with their peers. We see the weak areas we need to address in their lives. We try to keep them from situations where they will be confronted with evil.

We only have our children at home for a short time to raise and train properly. One day they will be out on their own and will have to discern and deal with evil appropriately. Until that time, it is our desire to teach them what is true, good, and proper. We want them to be so certain of what is right that they will easily identify wrong when they are older. The best way we know how to teach them these things is to keep them from evil while they are young. As parents we are responsible for those things that our children are exposed to as young people. May their experiences be those that bring glory to God and are not harmful to themselves.

Do you know where your children are and who they are with? What are they doing?

PRAYER

Father, thank You that we received strong teaching regarding sheltering our children while they were still young. It has been difficult to make this happen, but it was well worth it. Help me to continue to take the time to monitor the activities of my children as they get older. Let me not be naive in any possible situation and leave my children to themselves. ❧

FOOD FOR THOUGHT

1. Are you selective regarding what your children are exposed to in movies, television, and the Internet? What other areas warrant careful consideration?

2. Do your children soak in evil in ways you haven't considered, such as the evening news or newspaper?

3. Determine to teach your children truth while banishing evil from your home.

WHAT IS YOUR MOTIVATION?

Search me, O God, and know my heart: try me, and
know my thoughts: And see if there be any wicked way in me,
and lead me in the way everlasting.

PSALM 139:23-24

In the business world everyone is concerned with results. What is the bottom line? Many do not care how the results are achieved as long as they are there. I have worked for more than one company that had unethical business practices. I was fired from one job because I was asking too many questions about something that I later found out was illegal. My honesty was not compatible with their corporate practices.

Right results with the wrong motivation isn't necessarily right at all. It is possible that we are doing the right thing for the wrong reason, which will affect the outcome. Last summer we bought a share in a small CSA (Community Supported Agriculture) farm that grew organic vegetables. Thrilled with the prospect of finally finding an affordable source of healthy vegetables, I read their weekly newsletter with enthusiasm. We attended an open house at the farm. Early on we learned that the farmer and his workers, who all lived together at the farm, gave spiritual significance to the land and the vegetables. Our heavenly Father who created the land was conspicuously missing from their ideology. The land and the vegetables had become idols for them. I had other concerns, too, but this was enough to deter me from participating in the farm again. The vegetables were great, but the motivation of the people running the farm negatively affected the outcome for me.

Homeschooling is good. The results are superior. But it can be done for the wrong reasons. We do the good that we do as homeschool moms as an act of service to our Lord. Homeschooling is not a work to gain God's favor in the first place. Homeschooling is not done to help us earn our salvation. The fact that homeschooling is becoming popular is not a good reason to homeschool.

Our decision to homeschool grew out of our conviction that we are to raise our children in the fear and admonition of the Lord. Besides being the only way for *our* family to do this, we feel that it has been the best way. There are many motivations that turn a family toward homeschooling. It is important for the outcome of your efforts that your reasons are honoring to God.

Why do you homeschool? Are your motives just and good?

PRAYER

Father, it is so easy for me to have wrong thoughts. I am tempted daily to look at things from an earthly perspective. I want my motives behind homeschooling to be honoring to You. Keeping the favor of other homeschooling families is not the type of motivation You are looking for in me. Help me to see Your larger plan behind my feeble efforts. ❧

FOOD FOR THOUGHT

1. Write down all of the reasons why you homeschool. Reevaluate any that are not honoring to God.
2. Discuss together as a family the topic of family goals. Decide on a few goals to begin with to set the tone for your school.
3. Be prepared to answer those who ask you why you homeschool. Take their question as an opportunity to share the Gospel.

8 5

TELL ME THE TRUTH

*For kings, and for all that are in authority; that we may lead a
quiet and peaceable life in all godliness and honesty. For this is good
and acceptable in the sight of God our Savior; Who will have all men
to be saved, and to come unto the knowledge of the truth.*

1 TIMOTHY 2:2-4

I was interested in a new science magazine that I received information about
in a mass mailing. It looked interesting, but I could not tell if it was a Christian
publication. I called the telephone number of the distributor, and they did not
know. I then called the publisher and had a most interesting conversation
with the girl who worked in the office. When I asked if the magazine was writ-
ten from a creationist perspective, she was unable to answer clearly one way
or the other. Eventually she said that she would talk to the editor and call
me back later.

When the woman returned my call, we talked a few minutes, and I
related to her that we were Christians and believed that God created the
world. She asked me if I taught the children other views. The question seemed
odd to me because I don't consider truth to be a "view." Many people, however, do not hold fast to any truths and believe many views simultaneously.
They have no definitive belief in right or wrong. To them there are no
absolutes. This tendency is not compatible with biblical Christianity.

As we educate our children at home, we are committed to teaching
them the truth. A popular educational technique in our day is to teach chil-

dren everything and let them decide for themselves which is true. This is a most difficult way to learn to discern truth. Imagine the situation I would have if I taught them all about the major religions of the world and then asked them to tell me which one was right. Unless I present the Gospel of Jesus Christ to them clearly and they choose Jesus as their Savior, it will be almost impossible for them to process all of the other information correctly.

I am taking a more active role in teaching my children to discern error. My older daughters and son are reading the newspaper, and I listen for comments about what they read. I must teach them that not everything they read in a newspaper is true. What they hear on the radio during the news broadcast must be filtered through minds grounded in the Word of God so they can question what does not seem right to them.

Are you filling the minds of your children with truth? How about *your* mind?

PRAYER

Father, grant me a greater understanding of the Bible. Let me be an effective teacher of truth to my children. I pray that they would grow up to be wise men and women who know Your Word and apply it daily in their lives. May our home be a place of understanding Your truth. ❧

FOOD FOR THOUGHT

1. Do your children know the truth about Jesus Christ—His death, burial, and resurrection that paid the penalty for all of our sins?
2. Are godly character qualities being taught as a part of your core curriculum?
3. Teach your children to think critically when determining whether something is true or not.

8 6

HOW DO WE LOOK?

Prove all things; hold fast that which is good.
Abstain from all appearance of evil.

1 THESSALONIANS 5:21-22

&

I remember how I felt when we decided that the women in our family would wear dresses. I was uneasy. I wasn't sure how the people around me would respond. I wasn't sure I would always feel like wearing a dress. I liked wearing pants. I did not make the change overnight. It came gradually until one day it made perfect sense to me to just wear dresses. It felt good to have that settled in my mind, and I was finally at peace with our decision.

We did not make this decision in affiliation with any denomination or group. We simply were convicted in our reading of the Bible that modest dress for women would be a dress, skirt, or culottes. We studied the issue and prayed about it before making this decision. I struggled to find appropriate clothing in a culture where women wear pants and short skirts. We also decided that the women in our family would have long hair. Again this conviction came from our own reading of the Bible and was what God put on our hearts for our own family.

At the time I did not know it, but we were setting standards for our family. Based on the Bible, these decisions were for *us*. Those around us would have to decide for themselves. What a surprise it was to me to see that the wearing of dresses in our family became a point of discussion in the church and outside. Varied opinions were expressed about why we wore dresses, and it became a topic that really should not have taken on the importance that it did except for the fact that we had set a standard for our own family.

Setting standards in clothing, television viewing, movies, friendships, and other areas can bring division. Some will applaud you, and others will exclude you. The middle-of-the-roaders tolerate you even though they don't understand you. Having standards is good and desirable. The Bible is the source of godly standards. Make sure that standards are set for your family by the head of your family. Those outside your family should not be made to feel inferior because they do not share your standards. At the same time don't apologize for having convictions. Rest in knowing that godly standards are set in obedience to God's Word and are for the purpose of pleasing Him.

Do you have standards for your children? For your family?

PRAYER

Lord, thank You for guiding our family through Your Word to standards in our daily life. Show me best how to implement these successfully to Your glory. Help me to hold fast to our standard when the criticism comes. It is You we are pleasing anyway. ⊰

FOOD FOR THOUGHT

1. Have others criticized you for having standards? How have you responded?
2. Are there any practices in your household that have the appearance of evil? Get rid of them.
3. If an unsaved person looked at your family, would he or she see any differences between you and a non-Christian family? What is different? Is it something that encourages the observer to seek God or to flee from the church?

8 7

SIMPLE LIVING

And that ye study to be quiet, and to do your own business, and
to work with your own hands, as we commanded you; That
ye may walk honestly toward them that are without,
and that ye may have lack of nothing.

1 THESSALONIANS 4:11-12

I did not know what to expect when we signed up to spend a week on a
homestead learning more about living simply. The owners lived off their land,
and we wanted to pick up as much as we could from them so we could simplify our own life. Without running water or electricity in their home, it was
quite different from anything I had ever seen. After making some initial
adjustments to the sudden lack of facilities, I was able to gain a great deal of
information about doing things for yourself. Most striking was the new understanding I had of the beneficial nature of having a strong work ethic within
a family.

When you live off the land, you work or you don't eat. You get fire-
wood, or you don't get warm. Work is foundational to survival. I was taken
by the attitudes of their children toward work. They accepted it as a natural
part of their existence. We have decided to make this a goal for our own
family. From the time they are small, our children learn to work. We work
together and have fun in the process. Working in our home is normal for
the children. It is a natural part of their existence.

As we work together, we are able to provide for more of our own needs rather than having to depend on others. We have a garden, grind our own wheat, and have milk goats and chickens. It might seem that we work harder to have a simple lifestyle, and in some ways we do. But when it comes to interdependence with the intricate world systems, we aren't as involved as we used to be.

As complex world problems affect each individual more directly with each passing year, it makes sense to learn to work with your hands. Provide for your own family in ways that the world cannot take from you. Train your children to work hard and fill their heads with hundreds of useful skills to enhance their daily living.

Is your life too complicated? What can you change first?

PRAYER

Lord, thank You for showing me the value of a work ethic. I am grateful that we were able to instill such thoughts into our children while they were young. Our children love to work, and it is such a blessing to us. I am certain that it is a blessing to You when You see me working so hard. Keep me healthy and fit so that I may continue to work hard for the cause of Your kingdom. ❧

FOOD FOR THOUGHT

1. Do you train your children in developing specific skills? Do you have materials and equipment for them to use?

2. Do *you* need to develop new skills? See *The Busy Mom's Guide to Simple Living* (Crossway Books, 1997).

3. What advantages do you have when your family can provide more of its own needs? Is your family prepared to do so if challenging times lie ahead? What should you do to be more prepared for such a time?

YES, SIR!

Honor all men. Love the brotherhood. Fear God. Honor the king.

1 PETER 2 : 17

❧

We attended a church where one of the pastors continued to call me Mrs. Wellwood even after I asked him to call me by my first name. It made me feel strange, and it took some time for me to figure out why. It was because he was showing me respect, and this was not something that I had experienced much in our culture. I wasn't used to being treated this way. It seemed too formal to me when in reality it was just being polite. It is good when someone treats you with respect. It is excellent when children show respect to each other and to the adults around them.

Our two-year-old Josiah does a good job of showing respect. We have taught him how to do it. He has learned to answer with "yes, ma'am" or "yes, sir" when an adult is addressing him. A good portion of the time he answers correctly. This is not the case with our older children, who did not receive the same training. While they know how to respond correctly, they have to be reminded. It is more difficult for them to remember to answer politely because they have not made showing respect a habit.

Habits are not always bad. Most of our habits can and should be good ones. For example, we have instructed our boys to open doors for their sisters and mother. The males in our household stand at the table until all of the females have been seated. Dad opens the car door for Mom when we are out together. By teaching your children good habits that show respect for others, you are teaching them how to show honor.

Your good example in the area of showing respect is a very effective teacher. I am trying to say "yes, ma'am" and "yes, sir" to my children when I speak to them. I am trying to make this a habit in my own life. It is good for me to speak this way to everyone. Even if this is not the way most people talk, it is a good way to show honor to another person. As we honor each other, we show honor to God.

Are you polite to your children? To your husband?

PRAYER

Father, forgive me for my negligence. I have failed to train most of my children to show respect properly. I see now how much longer it takes when you don't teach it from the beginning. Forgive me also for neglecting to show my husband the respect that he deserves. It only follows that I am not showing You the respect that You are due either. Please show me how to do a better job in my own life. Help me to teach the children properly in such a critical area. Thank You for being patient with me. ❧

FOOD FOR THOUGHT

1. Do adult members of your family show respect to each other, providing a good example for the children?
2. Require your children from toddlerhood to show you respect. Practice appropriate responses when an adult talks to them. Praise them for showing respect.
3. Model respect by saying "yes, ma'am" and "yes, sir" to them.

8 9

I DID IT

He that covereth his sins shall not prosper: but whoso
confesseth and forsaketh them shall have mercy.

PROVERBS 28:13

I had a bad day today. My husband was working, so the children and I went to church alone. I was up with the baby and had not gotten enough sleep. When I woke up, I had a nasty sinus headache that would not quit. By the time we got home from church and got the meal on the table, I was feeling pretty bad. My patience level for childish antics was zero. My head was throbbing, and I struggled with all of the issues that go with one adult supervising a meal with many small children. By the time I was able to crawl off to bed for a nap, I had sinned.

A couple of the children had behavioral issues that needed to be addressed. I handled them badly. I raised my voice and only managed to get everyone upset. Just minutes ago when my ten-year-old Jenny was helping me start some laundry, I apologized to her for my behavior. I explained that my actions were due to a splitting headache. I essentially was telling her that I was justified in my sin because of the circumstances. It sounds good, but it just isn't true.

When we make excuses, we are covering our sins. Justifying sin by citing circumstances that caused us to do wrong prevents us from handling it properly. Rather than confess and repent, I was making excuses to Jenny for my behavior. No wonder my children do the same thing. How much worse when we sin at the end of a day when *their* disobedience has been our undoing.

If I have not addressed disobedience properly as it happened, by the end of the day I can be quite annoyed. I may raise my voice to them. While their disobedience requires correction, it does not excuse my own sinful behavior. Until I stop making excuses for what I am doing wrong, I won't make any progress in correcting it. There is no excuse for sin. It is wrong. If I am to prosper, then I must confess sin and deal with it. This is God's way. I must make it my way, too.

Do you justify your sin by citing extenuating circumstances? Does God?

PRAYER

Heavenly Father, forgive me for my sins. I don't like to call them that. The word seems too harsh. In reality I sin throughout the day, and I guess that fact is too much for me to face. Forgive me for teaching my children to excuse their own sin by my poor example. I have no choice but to get this right and be an appropriate model for my children. I want them to take ownership for their behavior. Help me, Lord, to break this ugly habit. ❧

FOOD FOR THOUGHT

1. Do you make excuses for your failures, or do you call sin what it is and deal with it? Confess your sins to the Lord and ask His forgiveness. Do this with your family also.

2. What do your children do when they fail? Teach them about forgiveness and repentance.

3. Memorize Proverbs 28:13 as a family. Hold each other accountable.

9 0

UNITED WE STAND

And Jesus knew their thoughts, and said unto them, Every kingdom divided against itself is brought to desolation; and every city or house divided against itself shall not stand.

MATTHEW 12:25

⋙

When our oldest was three years old, I was blessed with a husband who had a vision for our family. He approached me about homeschooling before I had even considered it. In submission to his wishes I got enough information to formulate my own opinion. I readily agreed to this type of education for our children. Before any steps were taken, we were both in agreement to proceed. If my husband had not supported homeschooling, then we would have had a different situation.

A number of women have shared their homeschooling struggles with me. Many have problems directly related to lack of support from their husbands. These husbands may have no interest in homeschooling or are possibly overwhelmed with a demanding job. Many times the problem is that the husband does not want the children homeschooled. If the wife persists in homeschooling under these terms, it will be on dangerous ground because they will have become a house divided.

Not all husbands warm up to homeschooling as quickly as their wives. This is true in many areas of life where a wife may see a need before her husband and must wait for him to see it, too. There is nothing wrong with starting to homeschool with a wait-and-see attitude. For all of us, the first year is a test. Husbands who are unsure but who decide that homeschooling is an option can turn into some of the greatest helpers along the way. Husbands who are opposed can change their minds, but homeschooling should not begin until that happens. If a wife thinks that homeschooling without her husband's blessing will somehow change his mind, she is missing the biblical principle of headship.

The husband is the head of the wife as Christ is the head of the church (Eph. 5:23). It will be your husband who will answer to God for your family. It is your husband who should decide if homeschooling fits in with his vision for your family. Public or private school with the husband's blessing is a better choice than the wife's homeschooling against the husband's wishes. A house divided will not stand.

How does your husband feel about homeschooling? Have you asked him lately?

PRAYER

Father, I am truly blessed. My husband has always been 100 percent in favor of homeschooling. Even when I have my doubts, he encourages me to continue. Thank You for his support. Please help women who don't have this situation to see the need to wait on their husbands. You truly do work through husbands even when it doesn't seem to make sense. Place a desire in the hearts of fathers for homeschooling. Give wives the courage to wait for the blessing of their husbands before beginning. ❧

FOOD FOR THOUGHT

1. Are both you and your husband behind homeschooling for your children? If not, you should go back to your husband and reconsider the schooling option that is best for your family.
2. Gently tell your husband what you need so he can better support you.
3. Periodically evaluate how both of you feel about the way homeschooling is working in your home. Foster unity of purpose before differences divide you.

9 1

COME ON OVER

*Be not forgetful to entertain strangers: for thereby
some have entertained angels unawares.*

HEBREWS 13:2

⁒

*F*or a number of months our family traveled quite a long distance to attend church on Sundays. The teaching was exactly the family-strengthening message we needed to hear. After two and a half years we were able to move close enough to become members of this church. Before we moved, we spent long afternoons at the church waiting for the evening service. We hardly knew anyone and did not really have anywhere to go. What blessings we received when a church member eagerly invited us over for a meal on the spur of the moment.

A single mother of two children on a limited income joyfully invited my family of seven to her home for Sunday dinner. I will never forget the sacrifice she made to include us that day. The meal was delicious and the fellowship special. She had us over a couple of times during our visiting months at the church. I wished I lived closer so I could see her more often. She was the first one I called when I found out that we were moving and we could indeed become better friends. It all started when she asked us over for a meal.

I love to have people in my home. Hospitality is a joy for me. It also takes work and commitment. It may mean sacrifice when finances are barely covering the food budget. Hospitality takes time. It may mean saying no to some activities so you can invite a family over. We schedule hospitality into our school schedule. Friday afternoons have traditionally been our time to invite families over for a visit. During the long winter months this can be the perfect end to a busy week indoors.

My children are included in the preparations to have others into our home. I want them to know how to be hospitable when they have families of their own. Preparations can be fancy or simple since the focus of the visit is the people. Dinner is not required. Asking a family over for dessert may be a good fit for both families. However it is done, the important thing is that it is done. My friend did not have to go to the trouble of serving a meal to a large family. But she did, and I have not forgotten the joy I saw in her face as she did it.

Have you had anyone over lately? Ask another homeschool family to come by for an afternoon.

PRAYER

Lord, thank You for the many people who have shown us hospitality. It motivates me to do the same. Please let me forget about spotless houses and empty calendars. Show me some time in each week to show someone hospitality. Expand my thinking so that I see more opportunities for fellowship with others. Thank You for sending angels in the form of strangers. Make me more inclined to invite those that I do not know so well to our home. ❧

FOOD FOR THOUGHT

1. What keeps you from inviting others to your home?
2. Change what you can about your circumstances, accept what you can't change, and invite people to your home.
3. Pray about whom you should invite each week.

DID YOU HEAR?

But let none of you suffer as a murderer, or as a thief, or as an evildoer, or as a busybody in other men's matters.

1 PETER 4:15

❧

*A*t times I have to point out to my children that they are being busybodies. It could be because they are making comments about their siblings' affairs that are none of their business. It might be that they have an opinion about what someone else is doing that is none of their concern. It may be that they are trying to tell me some news that belongs to another child. Sometimes they are just plain nosy when they hang around me when I am on the telephone. Children are not the only ones prone to being busybodies. Their mothers may set a bad example.

I don't ever intend to gossip, but I know there are times when I am a busybody. This usually happens when I get together with other women, and I am not careful about the subject matter I talk about. After spending so much time with children, it is easy for homeschool moms to unload the thoughts on our minds to another adult. Sometimes we say too much. We might say things about other people that do not build them up, but tear them down. We shouldn't be thinking these thoughts, let alone saying them aloud. We may share something that is going on in another family that we know about. The news is really not ours to report.

I also have to be careful that I do not share someone's good news with other people. It is their decision whom they want to tell. I should not be the town crier letting everyone know what is new. We all know someone like that.

She always knows what is going on in people's lives and freely tells all who will listen. She is a busybody. The Bible says she will suffer.

I don't want to suffer from being foolish when it comes to gossip. The only way I know how to keep this in check is to have criteria about what I should talk about. Even then I may walk a fine line. What I teach my children works well for me. Don't have an opinion about what people are doing. Keep your nose on your own business. Let others share their own news. Tell news only if it is your own.

Are you minding your own business? Should you be?

PRAYER

Father, create in me an awareness of what constitutes gossip. I don't want any part of it, but I believe I become a busybody when I don't understand what is appropriate for me to discuss and what is not. Keep me from these sins of ignorance. Help me to say only those things that build others up. Show me any areas where I fail in this regard. I want to please You. ❧

FOOD FOR THOUGHT

1. Do you tend to gossip? Confess this to the Lord and commit to talking only about your own business.
2. Look up the word *gossip* in the dictionary. Identify all areas of your life where this sin may need to be addressed.
3. Be careful not to be a hearer of gossip and so become part of the problem.

9 3

WHO IS YOUR MASTER?

And if it seem evil unto you to serve the Lord, choose you
this day whom ye will serve; whether the gods which your fathers
served that were on the other side of the flood, or the gods of
the Amorites, in whose land ye dwell: but as for me
and my house, we will serve the Lord.

JOSHUA 24:15

৵

Sometimes I get confused about whose expectations to meet. My husband, children, extended family, neighbors, church members, and friends all have expectations. Some of these conflict. It can be very difficult to sort through if you don't keep your eyes on the Lord. All that I do must be filtered through God's expectations of me. What would God's best be in a given situation? What would Jesus do?

When we first began to homeschool, we lived in a neighborhood where most of the women worked outside the home. When children turned three years old and could attend preschool, the mothers were pleased. Once the children were in first grade, the women in the neighborhood had the day to themselves or could work without arranging for childcare. It was expected that everyone would send the children off to school. But we didn't. We did not meet the expectations of the neighbors. Pretty soon it became obvious that we just did not fit in the neighborhood.

It is not unusual to run into conflicts when you fail to meet the expectations of others. People expect you to send your children to school just as they do. When you don't, it can trigger many thoughts in their minds. They may wonder if they are doing the wrong thing by sending their children to school. Just stirring up this doubt in their minds can strain your relationship. Often you won't even know what the problem is with another family that no longer seems friendly to you.

Ultimately the way you handle these conflicts will determine how successful you will be in God's eyes. It lies in knowing who it is you call your master. If God is the one who controls your life, then you must please Him with your decisions. If other people's opinions mean a lot to you, then you can expect that keeping everyone happy will be difficult, if not impossible. This does not mean that all Christians must homeschool. It does mean that if you are convicted that homeschooling is God's best for your own family, then you must do it without fear of the expectations of others.

Are you worried about what others think about homeschooling? Why?

PRAYER

Lord, thank You that I am learning to stop being a people-pleaser. Keeping people happy is much harder than simply following Your Word. You have made clear what You require of me. Grant me a sweet spirit when I fail to meet the expectations of others. Please prompt me when I fail to meet Yours. ✦

FOOD FOR THOUGHT

1. Do the expectations of others govern your choices? (This is not a problem if the one expecting you to do something is your husband.)
2. What do you do when your choices don't meet the expectations of others?
3. Commit your way to the Lord and follow wherever He leads you.

9 4

A PEACEFUL MOM

Peace I leave with you, my peace I give unto you:
not as the world giveth, give I unto you. Let not your
heart be troubled, neither let it be afraid.

JOHN 14:27

❧

I remember a day when my heart was troubled right in the middle of trying to work on schoolwork with the children. I was struggling with the logistics of the different needs of my children that all were clamoring to be met at once. I could not prioritize who needed me more, and I ended up feeling pulled in too many directions. Other concerns further distracted me from the children. Ineffective was the way I would have described myself that day because I lost control over the household.

It is so much easier to remain calm and peaceful when you are managing everything well. When you are in control, there is a sense of direction. When plans start to fall apart and things come up, it is more difficult to remain at peace. When relationships are strained and disappointments come, peace is tough to find. Peace is difficult to maintain when the challenges and concerns of each day consume you. Peace doesn't come to you automatically. Peace is something God leaves with you when you are in a right relationship with Him.

My oldest daughter Jamie remarked that our entire home is peaceful when I am peaceful. What a responsibility! This means that *I* am setting the tone for our home. No matter what storms may blow our way, it is Mom who calms the waters. Since I cannot begin to perform such a task on my own, I must rely on the Lord to keep me peaceful. Even as I write this devotional, I am experiencing difficulties in my life that make peace hard to attain for me. I pray for peace, and yet it does not come. There is only one reason I am struggling to keep a peaceful heart. After giving my cares to God, I keep taking them back. I keep mulling over my circumstances and feeling unsettled and upset.

A couple of days ago when I gave it all to the Lord, I felt at peace. Yesterday morning I felt peace as I prayed. I will have peace again today if I relinquish my right to try to understand my circumstances. When I just give it all over to Him, the peace returns. God's Word is true. He does not desire for my heart to be troubled nor for me to be afraid. I must take Him at His Word.

Is your heart troubled? Give it all to the Lord, quickly.

PRAYER

Father, help me. I don't understand how to feel peaceful in the midst of turmoil. I give You my cares, but I find myself calling them back. I don't have enough faith that You can handle it for me. Strengthen my faith and comfort my heart. I know You are there. ❧

FOOD FOR THOUGHT

1. Read the hymn "It Is Well with My Soul." Believe it!
2. List everything that keeps you from being at peace. Change what you can and give the rest to the Lord.
3. How do your children respond when you are at peace? Consider the profound impact that your gentle spirit can have on your family.

You Did It Again?

Take heed to yourselves: If thy brother trespass against thee, rebuke him; and if he repent, forgive him. And if he trespass against thee seven times in a day, and seven times in a day turn again to thee, saying, I repent; thou shalt forgive him.

LUKE 17:3-4

❧

*I*t is interesting to me how long it takes children to develop good habits. It seems that I teach them the same thing over and over again, and yet they still don't get it right. Instructions for kitchen cleanup are repeated daily as the same issues of the stove not being wiped, crumbs on the floor, and sloppily washed dishes come up at each meal. I begin to lose patience with this scenario. I wonder how many times I have to give the instructions before they are followed.

The answer is, as many times as it takes. I have made the mistake of giving directions and then expecting them to be followed. I did not check to see if they were satisfactorily completed. This may work on a job with trustworthy employees, but children are still in training. They need consistent follow-up in all areas of life. If I require clean bedrooms and beds made before breakfast, then I have to check to be sure that this is done. Eventually I won't need to follow up, but this will be later on.

As I follow up and find work done in a sloppy fashion, I need to address this with my child. If he is careless with his math problems and he is sorry, I need to forgive him. If he does the same thing tomorrow and the next day, I need to forgive him again. While what I am asking of my child may seem simple to me, it may be a great challenge to him. I have to be consistent to be sure he is diligent to do the job right. When I fail to be consistent, I prolong the time it takes for my child to learn what is right.

I get frustrated having to go over things so many times with my children. But imagine how God feels having to deal with me over and over again. How many times have I known exactly what God requires of me, and yet I have done the opposite? How does He feel? I know He does not lose His patience. And He does most certainly provide more and more opportunities for me to learn what He is trying to teach me. He never gives up, and sometimes He intensifies the lesson. We can do the same with our children.

Have you been consistent with your children today? Begin now.

PRAYER

Lord, You are such a role model for me regarding consistency. I desire to be consistent with my children. Help me to overcome the obstacles I face each time I try but fail. Remind me of how slow I am to learn some things when my patience with them is wearing thin. ❧

FOOD FOR THOUGHT

1. What keeps you from being consistent? Can you make improvements in this area?
2. Is the lack of consistency we see in our children a result of our own failure to be consistent? Ask God to help you to be more consistent.
3. Do you forgive your children when they struggle in the area of being consistent?

9 6

BABIES

And they brought young children to him, that he should touch them;
and his disciples rebuked those that brought them.

MARK 10:13

❧

*B*abies like to be touched. They like to be held. They thrive on love and attention. My six-month-old, Julianne, is her very happiest when someone is holding her. We may have spoiled her a bit by holding her so much as a newborn. I don't mind, because I believe in holding them as much as they want when they are infants. Once they crawl and then walk, they don't really spend much time on Mom's lap anymore. I know—the other six were that way. So I let them cuddle in my lap long and often when they are little.

Julianne feels secure and comforted when I hold her. I wonder if this was the same effect that Jesus had on the little children that He touched? Why did their parents feel it was important for Jesus to touch their children? Jesus knew that touch was good for children, and His model is one we should follow. How, then, do we teach our other children when we have a baby?

It is a challenge. For some moms, it is easier to sit down with the older children when the baby is asleep. I did this initially, but now I have so many children that it isn't that simple. I have had to adopt a philosophy that would have worked well even with a couple of children. Include the baby. Make the baby a part of whatever is going on in your school. Infants can sit on your lap while you teach or read a story aloud to the other children. Toddlers can have quiet toys to play with during school time. It takes an extra effort to teach this way, but the payback is worth it. Your small children will learn to sit quietly in church at a young age. They will learn to behave properly because you are being forced to take the time to train them right when they are very little.

Children need meaningful touch from their parents. It should not end when they begin to walk. All of my children need my hugs and kisses. All of my children benefit from a loving touch on the hand from Mom. Jesus showed us that children were important to Him. He touched them and loved them. This should be part of our curriculum.

Have you hugged your children today? Do it again.

PRAYER

Father, I confess that I find it easy to hold my babies, but I forget to hug and kiss my children as they get older. They need this from me, and I don't know why I don't do it more. Help me to develop the habit of giving my children meaningful touch. A pat on the back for my boys means so much. Let this be more natural for me. ❧

FOOD FOR THOUGHT

1. Do you prefer to schedule school around naps for little ones so they do not interrupt? Could both of you benefit from teaching them to sit on your lap while you instruct older children?

2. Make a list of all the things you *could* do with a baby on your lap. Put a star by those you are willing to try.

3. Praise God for your babies.

9 7

I'M HIDING

O Lord, thou hast searched me, and known me. Thou knowest my downsitting and mine uprising; thou understandest my thought afar off.

PSALM 139:1-2

◈

I have been known to take a little extra time in the bathroom. The truth be known, I'm hiding. I'm hiding from anyone who might watch me and evaluate what I am doing. I'm hiding from anyone who might need me—right now! I'm hiding from my two-year-old's whining. I'm hiding so I can eat the last chocolate chip cookie. I'm hiding from anything else that I need a break from—just a short one. Even five minutes of hiding can do wonders.

I feel a little uncomfortable being so vulnerable to my family. They see me all day long complete with all of my flaws. Nothing, it seems, can go by undetected. If I want a little snack (perfectly normal for a nursing mother), there is an army watching me waiting for theirs. If I want to take a few minutes to look at the newspaper, they read over my shoulder. If my character is less than what I am teaching them to be, I can tell just by looking at their faces. If I want to sneak a cookie right before dinner, I have to be extra sneaky to get away with it. I am under twenty-four-hour surveillance, it seems.

I really can hide from my family even if it is just for a few minutes. If I don't want them to know what I am thinking or see an impulsive reaction to something, I can slip away to somewhere in the house. But what about God? Doesn't He see *everything*? He knows what I am thinking. He knows every wrong motive I have. He knows where I will fail next. So why hide? It makes no sense really. We often try to keep a distance between ourselves and God so that He won't see what is wrong with us. At least we think we can hide.

If God knows all there is to know about us, then He is the one who can help us. While it is our natural inclination to turn away from people when we want to hide something, it should be our inclination to turn toward God for help. There is no hiding from God. If God is all-knowing (and He is), then this truth should impact me far more than realizing that my child is standing behind me watching me sneak another cookie. God knows of our needs before we even ask. There is no hiding.

Have you asked God for help? He won't hide from you.

PRAYER

Lord, it is foolish of me to think I can hide from You. Why would I want to do such a silly thing when You are the source of all help? Clear my thinking so I remember that You are my friend and will not turn me away in my hour of need. Thank You for never hiding Yourself from me. ❧

FOOD FOR THOUGHT

1. What (or whom) are you hiding from? Why?

2. Do you believe God is all-knowing? Then why do you try to hide from Him?

3. Honestly approach the throne of grace and confess your failures. Become transparent in front of your family.

9 8

KNOWLEDGE INTO ACTION

Therefore to him that knoweth to do good,
and doeth it not, to him it is sin.

JAMES 4:17

❧

I love to buy books. I have learned so much from books that I am excited by new ones on topics I haven't yet mastered. Reading books is a lifetime interest of mine. I own books that I know I can't get to now but plan to pursue later. By reading so much, I have gained much knowledge. Knowledge is good and helpful when it is applied properly to the situations of life. But I'm afraid that so much of what I have read is still head knowledge. I'm not sure I should buy any more books.

Even if I only owned a Bible, there is enough knowledge there to keep me busy forever. While I have studied the Bible and have a good understanding of its principles, I find that my knowledge too often fails me when it is time to turn what I know into action. Knowledge must travel from the mind all the way down into the heart to be truly useful. Watch your actions and reactions to see if this has happened in your life. When the children irritate you, do you respond with a sharp word spoken in haste, or do you stop a moment and deal with the situation properly? If schoolwork is not done well and on time, how do you react? Do you find that the way you act in your home is different from the way you act at church?

Head knowledge is pretty easy to teach to your children. Give them some books. Make some assignments. Grade some papers. They either get it or they don't. Heart knowledge is a little more difficult to instill in your children, but this knowledge is best. One way to evaluate heart knowledge is to watch how your children treat each other. Are they polite to adults? Do they follow house rules, or do they have to be prodded daily?

It is vital that we make sure that our children not only *know* what is right but *do* what is right. We must raise children of godly character, not children who are merely filled with facts. Head knowledge without heartfelt action is pretty useless. Knowledge becomes real when we use it. Be sure to teach your children in such a way that they know how to use what they know for the glory of God. It humbles me to realize that when I know to do good but don't do it, I sin. Our children should learn this, too.

Where is your knowledge? In your head or in your heart?

PRAYER

Dear Lord, thank You for granting me the ability to understand many things. I pray that You would refine my ability to apply what I know properly in daily life. Show me the best way to teach my children so they will have heart knowledge that shows itself in appropriate actions. May they do a better job than I do. ✎

FOOD FOR THOUGHT

1. What methods will transfer head knowledge into heartfelt action?
2. Limit the seeking of more information before you put what you already know into practice.
3. Do your children behave in ways that confirm that they understand how to apply what they are learning? Praise them when they do this well.

99

YES, MOMMY IS CRYING

They that sow in tears shall reap in joy.

PSALM 126:5

❧

I don't remember any of my public school teachers crying. I don't usually cry either while teaching my children, but I remember one time when
it came down to tears. I had been struggling all year with teaching one of
my daughters how to keep track of her assigned work and complete it on
time. Each week we had the same problem—the work was not complete. In
frustration I finally had a good cry. I had tried everything, and nothing
worked. I asked my husband to finish out the school year with her. I didn't
know what else to do. I just needed to step back from the situation for a
little while.

The time will come when she will get this right. There will be a time of
rejoicing for both teacher and student. At times I get discouraged and wonder if there will ever be any breakthroughs. I lose sight of the goal. Teaching
reading can bring the same disheartening feelings when it takes so long for
our dear student to understand the sounds of the letters. Children that have
learning disorders or are developmentally delayed require extra patience as
they try to grasp what they are being taught.

I don't expect all of my children to catch on to everything quickly. Some
will struggle with reading, and others will be stumped by math. It is important to see our children as individuals and not to compare them. Their
progress is more important than perfection. If we teach to a child's strengths,
then naturally some will go further in an area than another. There can be

moments of despair when after much hard work there is no progress. As homeschool moms we feel personally responsible. They are *our* children. We may feel like crying.

I am glad that I am getting such an up-close and personal look at the weaknesses in each of my children. If they were in another school setting, I might very well miss any opportunity to strengthen these weak areas because I would not be aware of them. A classroom teacher has many students and would likely not see all that I can see. But I do see their weaknesses, and because I desire the best for my children, I can easily strive for perfection in all areas. If I do, it will be easy to become discouraged when it doesn't come. A more worthy goal would be improvement in the weak areas. Rather than being consumed by my tears, I can shout with joy because I am able to help my children develop skills to overcome weak areas. That achievement will serve them throughout life.

Are you frustrated to tears? It's okay.

PRAYER

Father, I have some frustrating times when my children just don't understand their lessons. You know all about this because of the many times I have not learned Your lessons. When my children struggle with a concept, remind me of how long it has taken me to learn Your ways and exhibit greater patience. ❧

FOOD FOR THOUGHT

1. Are your expectations of your children too high? Your expectations of yourself?

2. Find a homeschool mom who has successfully overcome the same type of problem you are experiencing. Have her describe the process for you.

3. Pour out your tears to God. He understands.

100

TRANSITION

But I say unto you, That every idle word that men shall speak, they shall give account thereof in the day of judgment. For by thy words thou shalt be justified, and by thy words thou shalt be condemned.

MATTHEW 12:36-37

৵৶

I have given birth seven times. Each time a stage of labor came that I found particularly difficult—transition. That relatively short period of time just before the baby's delivery was the most difficult. Intense and uncomfortable, it could easily have been a time for me to say the wrong thing. I could have lost control and made some very damaging remarks. Fortunately this did not happen.

During other times of transition I did not fare as well, however. For me, moving was stressful, and I did not handle it well. I don't like transitions. Childbirth, moving, or any type of change can create that time of transition. Transition is unpleasant, and I can't do anything about it. My usual routines or methods don't work. I feel lost—out of control. But this time passes, and I get going again. It is not surprising that our children have transitional times, too.

Toddlers have so much on their minds but don't have the verbal skills to express themselves well enough to be understood. Two-year-old Josiah ends up screaming in frustration when nobody understands what he wants. His behavior requires correction, but he also needs understanding of the difficulty that accompanies being misunderstood all day. Children learning phonics but who are still unable to read are in a transitional phase. Our six-year-old Jonathan is frustrated during our family devotions because he can't read his Bible yet. When Dad calls for questions, Jonathan picks a verse by number to be explained. This is disappointing for him. He would rather be reading the verses like the older children.

Adolescence is a time of transition. Courtship is a final transition to life away from Mom and Dad. During these times we must be careful about what we say. During transitional times we may be more likely to say the wrong things because we are under stress. Wrong speech is always wrong. It is just more likely to occur during a transition. Therefore we must be on guard during this time to keep ourselves from sinning with our mouths. We must give an account for every word we say, be it good or bad. I prefer for my good words to far outweigh the bad ones. I want to be justified by my words and not condemned.

Are you in transition? How are you handling it?

PRAYER

Dear Lord, You have given me many opportunities to experience transitional times. They are stressful, and I have said things that I regret during them. Please help me to choose my words carefully. I want to use words to edify, not tear down. Show me how to teach my children to handle transitions in a godly way. ❧

FOOD FOR THOUGHT

1. How do you respond to times in your life that could be termed transitions?
2. Transitional times are for a limited period of time. Remember this!
3. *Expect* transition and lower your expectations for these times. Visualize other transitions that ended and remember how your life got back to normal.

1 0 1

WHAT DO THEY SEE IN ME?

He that saith, I know him, and keepeth not his commandments,
is a liar, and the truth is not in him.

1 JOHN 2:4

I was a little nervous after reading an article in the *Chicago Tribune* about our family. It was an excellent article that identified us as Christians. There were a number of pictures, and I knew that for a time people might recognize us. This did happen, and I am thankful that our family had a good testimony in public. Great!

But what about our family at home? How did we treat each other? How did Mom respond to Dad? Was Dad a good role model? It doesn't matter to our children what our family image is in public. What they see at home is our testimony. We are not the perfect family. We probably have an above average number of flaws in our family life. But our children know we are saved by the blood of Jesus Christ. They know that we are doing our best to follow biblical principles. We regularly need to make changes so that our walk is closer to Jesus. They see what we value and how we make our decisions. Still we deal with sin daily as we stray from the truth.

Our testimony is not how perfect we can appear to others. Our testimony is who we really are deep down inside. The mistakes (sins) we make don't have to discount us as Christians. Our failures give us an opportunity to behave like Christians when we deal with them. If I get off track with my daily devotions and give my children the impression that it really doesn't matter, then I have lost my testimony to them. They need to know what is right, and if I am not a good role model, then I need to be. I cannot afford to make excuses for failing to follow the Bible.

I wonder what my children would answer if someone asked them if I am following Christ or following my flesh. Do they see me making good decisions? Do I relate to other people properly? Do I follow biblical principles or merely talk about them?

What do your children see in you? Do they see Christ?

PRAYER

Heavenly Father, help me. I feel so small and weak. My example to my children of how a Christian should behave is woefully lacking today. Grant me a humble heart that readily admits my failures to them. Help me correct the wrongs and be a good testimony to them. Please use me in spite of my flaws to influence them for You. May their hearts be turned toward You and their desires be to please You. Shape me into a godly woman for the sake of my family. ❧

FOOD FOR THOUGHT

1. Reflect over the past week. Who has seen you or your family and been influenced by what they saw? There are probably many more of these people than you know.

2. Confess all of your failures (sins) right now and pray for your children to have open hearts to do the same. Ask each other for forgiveness.

3. Teach your children that their behavior is an influence on others either for good or for evil. Focus on practical ways to be a good influence.

If this book has blessed you and you would like to write me a note, or if you wish to contact me for availability to speak at a conference, I can be reached at:

EQUIPPING THE FAMILY
Attn: JMW
P. O. Box 458
Gridley, IL 61744-0458
(309) 747-4400

Personal Reflections